"This is a must-read for every high school graduate in America. Pat Williams shares all they will need for a lifetime of success."

—MIKE DAVIS, HEAD BASKETBALL COACH, INDIANA UNIVERSITY

"Pat Williams has composed an amazing set of principles and stories on which to build a successful life. He will challenge you to see through the shallow definitions of success and seek true greatness!"

—RON LUCE, PRESIDENT, TEEN MANIA MINISTRIES AND ACQUIRE THE FIRE EVENTS

"On the road to adulthood, consider this book your atlas. You'll find that fame and fortune aren't what they're cracked up to be if they're your only focus. Pat Williams has delivered a book loaded with wisdom on where your priorities lie, what truly matters, and how to live life to its fullest—and it all starts with having a Christ-centered, not a me-centered, life. Get this book for your son or daughter—but make sure you read it, too!"

—ERNIE JOHNSON, JR., SPORTSCASTER FOR TNT AND TBS

"Pat Williams knows something about success and winning. It's rare to find an adult that can communicate hard-learned lessons to students in a way that's both interesting and helpful. If you are a student, listen to this man. He knows what he's talking about."

—DAN WEBSTER, FOUNDER, AUTHENTIC LEADERSHIP, INC.

"With great clarity and passion, Pat Williams weaves together personal insights and powerful illustrations from the world of sports and business to offer solid advice that will serve graduates well as they set a course for the future."

"In *Play to Win,* Pat Williams gives graduates precisely the kind of solid advice they need to set a course for future success. This book brings a powerful message from a man who knows what true success is all about."

"*Play to Win* is clear on principles, long on inspiration. The best, however, is how you can decide to be successful in both this world and in your life forever with the Master Coach."

"I know all about fortune, pain, power, and pleasure— and believe me, the answers to life aren't found in any of those things. Pat Williams tells the truth in this important book that will change your future and help you find true success."

"With great clarity and passion, Pat Williams weaves together personal insights and powerful illustrations from the world of sports and business to offer solid advice that will serve graduates well as they set a course for the future."

PLAY 2 WIN

(FOR GUYS)

STRATEGIES FOR SUCCESS

IN THE GAME OF LIFE

PAT WILLIAMS

WITH DAVID WIMBISH

Baker Books

A Division of Baker Book House Co
Grand Rapids, Michigan 49516

Published by Baker Books
a division of Baker Book House Company
P.O. Box 6287, Grand Rapids, MI 49516-6287
www.bakerbooks.com

Printed in the United States of America

Library of Congress Cataloging-in-Publication Data

Williams, Pat, 1940–
    Play to win (for guys) : strategies for success in the game of life /
Pat Williams with David Wimbish.
        p. cm.
    Summary: A collection of Biblical truths, practical wisdom, and
    true stories of popular athletes to inspire high school graduates
    to find success by following a life of faith.
        ISBN 0-8010-4502-9
        1. Young men—Religious life. 2. College graduates—Religious
    life. 3. High school graduates—Religious life. 4. Success—Reli-
    gious aspects—Christianity. [1. Success—Religious aspects—
    Christianity. 2. Conduct of life. 3. Christian life.] I. Wimbish,
    David. II. Title.

    BV4541.3 .W55 2003
    248.8′32—dc21   2002012676

This book is dedicated with much love and pride to my daughter

Kati, a young lady who learned very early in life

the importance of ''playing to win.''

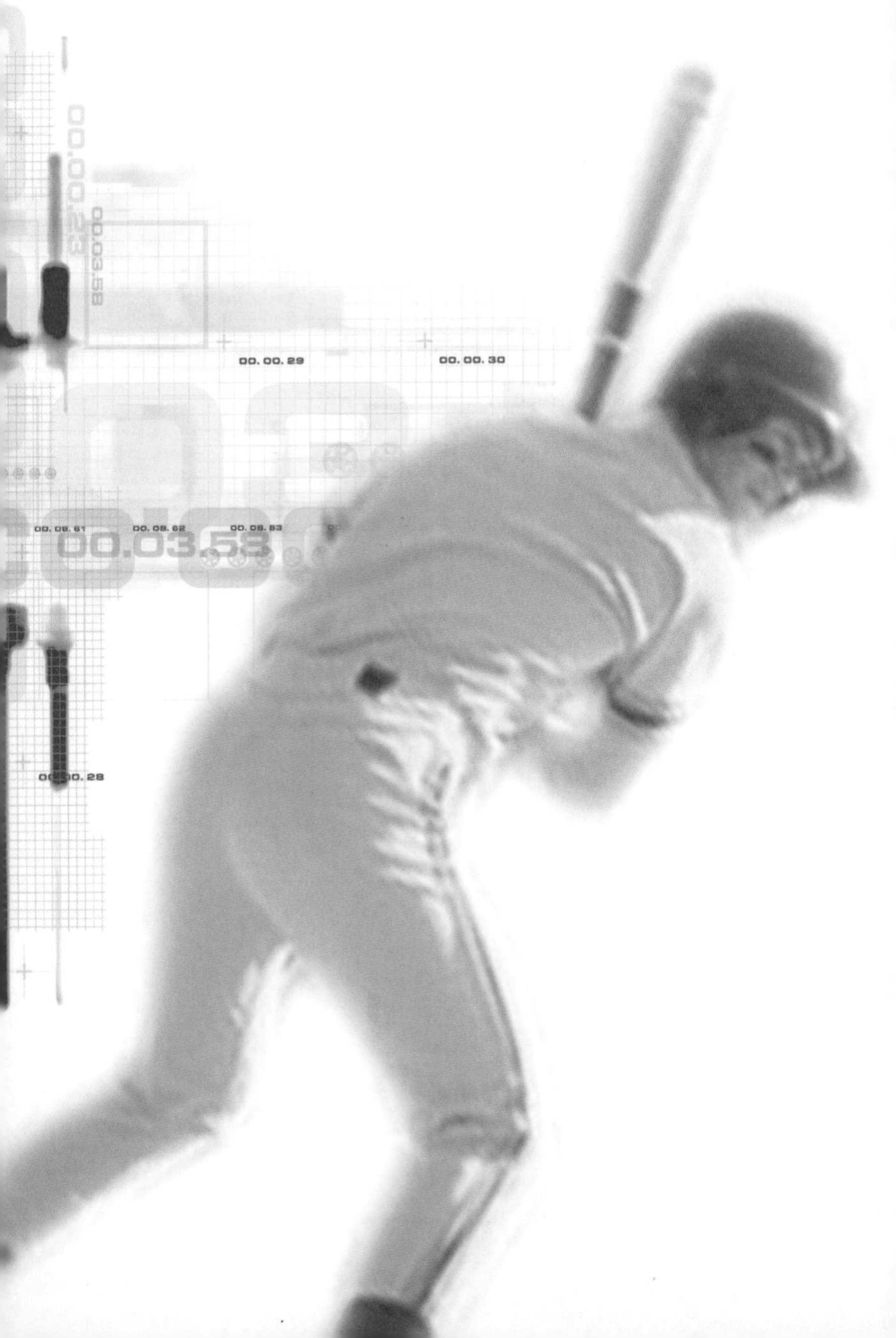
00.00.29
00.00.30
00.03.58

CONTENTS

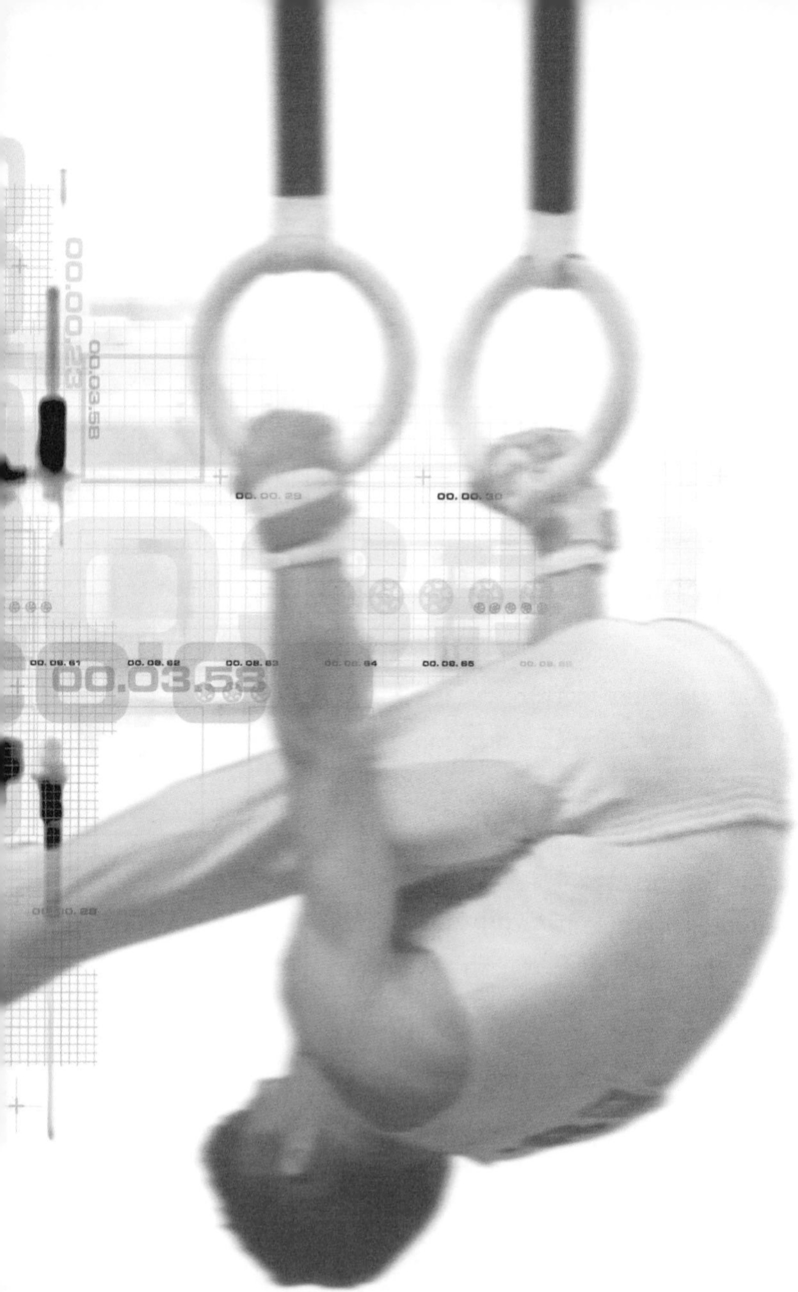
00.03.58

ACKNOWLEDGMENTS

IT IS WITH DEEP APPRECIATION that I acknowledge the support and guidance of the following people:

Special thanks go to Bob Vander Weide and John Weisbrod of the RDV Sports family. Thanks to my assistant, Melinda Ethington, for all that you do and continue to do. Hats off to Hank Martens of the RDV Sports mail room, a very dependable associate. Hearty thanks are also due to the staff at Baker Book House, and to my cohort in writing this book, David Wimbish. Thank you for believing that I had something important to say and for providing the forum to say it. Thank you to proofreader extraordinaire Ken Hussar, and to Mike Sweeney for writing the foreword. And finally, special thanks and appreciation go to my wife, Ruth, my most valuable assistant in life and in all phases of this book. I love you, Ruth!

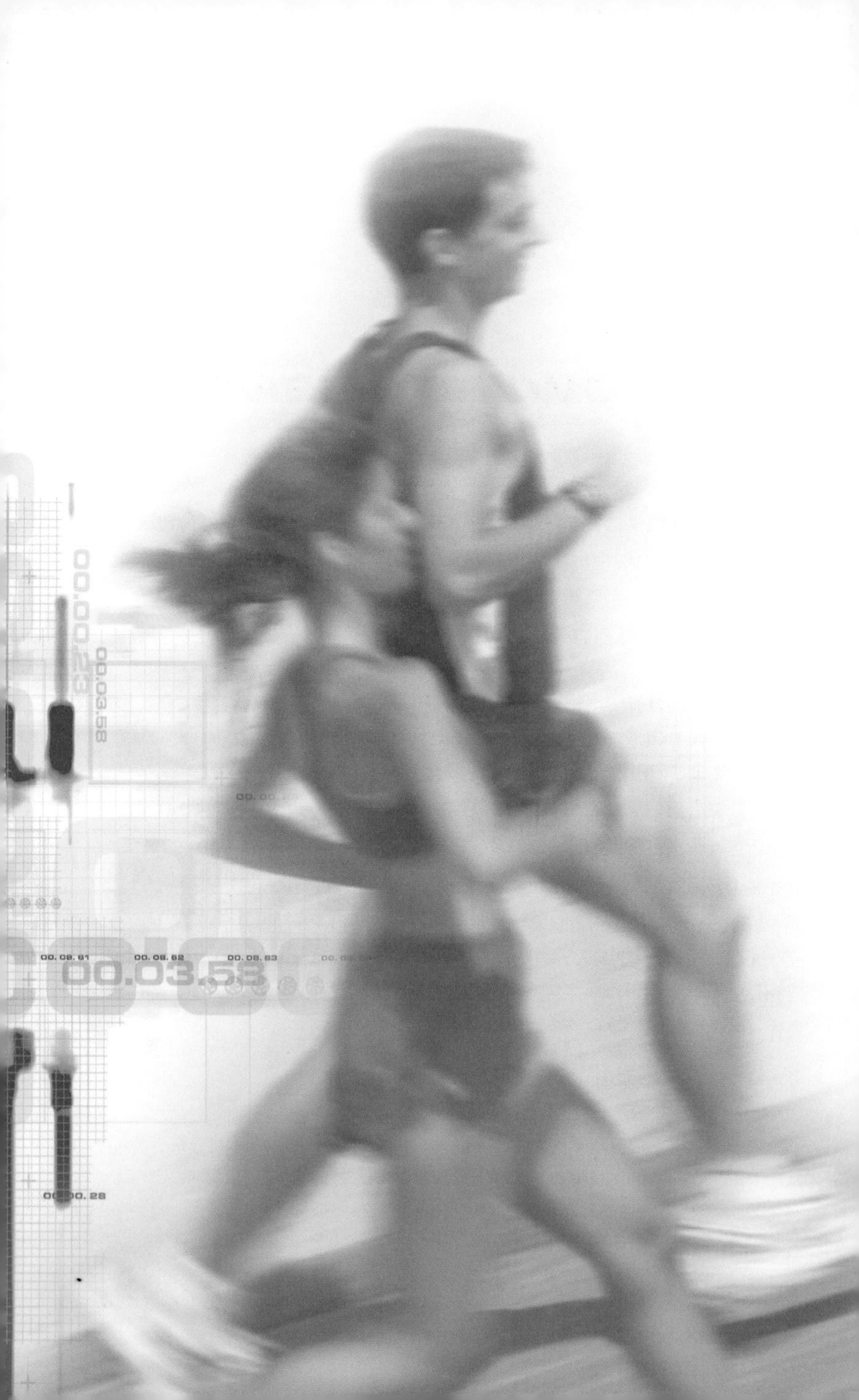
00.03.58

FOREWORD

HAVE YOU EVER THOUGHT about what it means to be truly successful in life?

If so—and if you're a guy who loves baseball, like me— you might be tempted to think that success is being on a major league roster. That *is* a wonderful thing, but it's not something you can build an entire life around.

How about knocking in 144 runs, like I did for the Kansas City Royals during the 2000 season? Nope.

Hitting .304 with 29 homers, like in 2001? Nah.

As proud as I am of those statistics, who will remember them 50 years from now? The fact is, there's more to life than playing professional sports. There's more to life than applause, fame, money, or any of the things most people think will make them happy.

You see, success is a personal relationship with Jesus that brings joy and contentment to your life. And that's why I'd consider myself successful even if I was stuck in AA and couldn't get my batting average above .200!

If you want to know more about what it means to be successful, just keep reading the book you're holding in your hands. My friend Pat Williams knows all about success, and he's going to tell you almost everything he knows!

MIKE SWEENEY, AMERICAN LEAGUE ALL-STAR

INTRODUCTION

Try first to be a man of value.
Success will follow.

ALBERT EINSTEIN

IT WAS A STUPID IDEA.

Just about everyone agreed with that. Just about everyone also agreed that Michael Jordan had been the best basketball player who'd ever lived. But his basketball-playing days were in the past. Why in the world would he want to come out of retirement at the "ripe old age" of thirty-eight?

Sports experts everywhere shook their heads and urged Jordan to change his mind. He'd been out of the game for several years. Surely his skills had diminished during that time. "Leave us with our great memories of you," they begged him. "Don't make us feel sorry for you by watching you try to keep up with men who are fifteen years younger than you." After all, Michael Jordan had already done everything a man could possibly do on a basketball court. He'd earned scoring titles, Most Valuable Player awards, and a fistful of NBA championships with the Chicago Bulls. There was nothing left to prove.

And when the 2001–2002 NBA season began, it seemed all of those "experts" had known what they were talking about. In one game, Jordan missed 75 percent of his field-goal attempts. His new team, the Washington Wizards, lost seven of their first eight contests.

Michael Jordan's comeback looked like a complete failure.

But Jordan kept on trying, and eventually things started falling into place. He began hitting from all over the floor. And the Wizards began winning.

As it turned out, the team didn't set any records—but they had their best season in years. And although Jordan's comeback was interrupted by knee surgery, he proved that even at age thirty-nine he could be a dominant presence in the NBA.

If you read the sports pages in your local newspaper or listen to sports talk radio, you'll have a difficult time finding anyone who admits they had doubts about Jordan's comeback. But the truth is, the only one who never had any doubts was Michael Jordan himself. And he was the only one who really mattered.

I can't tell you that *I* expected Michael Jordan's comeback to be so successful. But as someone who has known Jordan for years, I'm not surprised. I know his talent, his determination, and his work ethic. If somebody were to ask me what it takes to be a success in the world of sports, I'd point to Michael Jordan.

Or I'd point to someone like the late Florence Griffith Joyner, who was the first American woman to win four medals at an Olympic competition. Flo Jo, who passed away several years ago, took three gold medals and one silver medal at Seoul in 1988.

I've experienced many thrills in my life, and one of them was getting to sit next to Flo Jo at the Touchdown Club Awards Dinner in 1995. During the course of our conversation, Flo Jo told me about when she was a child growing up in a poor family (with eleven children!) in South Central Los Angeles. "I didn't have much going for me," she said. "In fact, you'd have to say that there was not much of a future for me."

But when she was eight years old, she had the privilege of meeting Sugar Ray Robinson, the great boxing champion. "Sugar Ray looked me right in the face," Flo Jo said. "He told me, 'It doesn't matter where you come from, what your color is, or what the odds are against you. What does matter is that you have a dream, that you believe you can do it, that you commit to doing it. It *can* happen, and it *will* happen!'" She went on, "Right there, at just eight years old, I was sold. I was all fired up about what my future could be."

Despite the odds against her, Flo Jo believed in a dream and rose to be the best in her field, setting world records in the one-hundred-meter and two-hundred-meter events. What's more, she was a beautiful, gracious, and humble woman who did everything she could to help those who needed a little bit of encouragement to pursue their own dreams.

And then there's Lou Holtz.

Like Michael Jordan, he knows what it's like to have people shake their heads and say, "He must be out of his mind!" That's what they did when he took the position of head football coach at the University of South Carolina.

By anybody's standards, Holtz had already enjoyed a long and successful career as a football coach. He'd been a winner everywhere he'd gone, including the University of Notre Dame.

But South Carolina? The Gamecocks had a losing tradition stretching as far back as anyone could remember. Winning seasons occurred with roughly the same frequency as snowfalls in Phoenix. Holtz was only a few years away from retirement, and it was going to be really sad to see him finish at the bottom.

During his first year as coach, the Gamecocks didn't win a game. And they not only lost—they lost big! Some people expected Holtz to admit he'd made a mistake and walk away from the team. But instead, he stayed around for a second year of punishment.

And then a strange thing happened. South Carolina started winning. After four or five wins in a row, even Holtz's harshest critics had to admit he'd turned South Carolina into one of the best college football programs in the country. What's more, his teams have kept on winning, and they've been ranked in the top twenty ever since.

Why am I talking so much about Michael Jordan, Florence Griffith Joyner, and Lou Holtz? Because they are just three of the many people who've shown me what it means to be a success in life. In this book, I want to share with you how these people made it to the top. And how they stayed there.

I'm talking about people like Tara VanDerveer, the women's basketball coach at Stanford University, who said, "What I have discovered over the years is that success is rooted not only in confidence and hard work, but in joy. Passion produces its own energy."

And Berry Gordy, founder of the multibillion-dollar Motown music empire, who wrote:

Unless you consider happiness before you consider success, the manner in which you achieve success could be something that would destroy you later. Many people are so busy running to the top, stepping on their competitors, stepping on their enemies and, saddest of all, stepping on their friends and loved ones, that when they get to the top, they look around and discover that they are lonely and unhappy. They'll ask me, "Where did I go wrong?" My answer has always been, "Probably at the beginning."

Before we go on with our discussion about success, I want to ask you a very important question.

Are you scared?

I was, when I was your age. I was scared because I wasn't sure what the future was going to bring my way. Because I had dozens of difficult decisions to make, and I was afraid of making the wrong ones. But mostly because I knew the time had come for me to "sink or swim" on my own. And despite all the confidence some people seemed to have in me, I wasn't really sure I could swim. In fact, I was under so much self-imposed pressure that I don't remember getting one good night's sleep my entire senior year of high school. At the time, I didn't have a deep faith in God to sustain me, and the future looked very scary.

I went to an excellent prep school in Wilmington, Delaware—an institution with a strong emphasis on academics. I was pretty good on the baseball diamond; I wasn't so hot in the classroom. My baseball coach, Tom Hartmann, was a Princeton graduate, and he assumed everyone else wanted to go to Princeton too. I'll never forget when he told my mother, with great compassion in his voice, "Ellen, I don't think Pat's going to be able to go to Princeton."

That certainly didn't come as any surprise to me—or to my mother!

Nevertheless, I had a dream, and I was determined to pursue it. I *didn't* go to Princeton, as it turned out. But I was accepted into another fine university—Wake Forest. I did okay there. And you know what? I've done okay since then too!

But I still remember the fears of that senior year in high school—fears that were made worse when people I respected and admired didn't seem to believe in me. If you're not bothered by fears like that, congratulations! You have a healthy self-confidence that will serve you well in life.

But if you're like most people I know, you're well acquainted with anxiety. No matter how frightened or insecure you may feel right now, I want you to know that God has given you all the tools you need to be a great success in life. All you have to do is learn how to use those tools properly.

Yes, I understand you have grown up in a world plagued by war, crime, and economic uncertainty. But even in today's difficult atmosphere, you can have a life that brings you personal satisfaction, fulfillment, and joy.

Are you ready? Let's roll!

ONE

SUCCESS

THE STUFF DREAMS ARE MADE OF

*For every human there is a quest
to find the answer to "Why am I
here? Where did I come from?
Where am I going?" For me, that
became the most important
thing in my life. Everything else
is secondary.*

GEORGE HARRISON, FORMER BEATLE

IF YOU'RE READING THIS BOOK, you've probably just graduated from high school or college. I'm almost certain that one of your graduation speakers said something about this occasion being not an end, but a beginning. And so it is.

You're about to set out on an incredible journey that will most likely last for the next sixty or seventy years (and even beyond that into eternity). Your generation will change the world, for better or for worse. In fact, I believe that you personally have the ability to change the world in some important way. That's why it's crucial to get off to a good start, to be sure that the first few steps you take are pointed in the right direction.

An acquaintance of mine works for the Jet Propulsion Laboratory in Pasadena (they're the folks who build most of our country's satellites and space probes). He recently told me that if there is one tiny error in the calculations at the beginning of a space flight—an error of a fraction of an inch or one decimal point—by the time the spacecraft reaches its destination, it will be hundreds, perhaps even thousands, of miles off course. Yes, little things do count. And the little things you do today will make a tremendous difference tomorrow.

THE BEST IS YET TO COME

Has anyone ever told you that someday you'll look back on high school as the best years of your life?

Baloney! Don't you believe it.

If anybody had told me *that* when I was in high school, I would've gotten depressed. Not that I didn't have plenty of good times when I was a teenager. I did. But I also had my share of problems and stress, and the idea that everything was going to go downhill would've been hard to take.

Of course, maybe high school has been great for you. You've been a star student, a top athlete, and way up there on the list of the most popular kids in school. But no matter how much fun you've had during the past four years, I want you to know that your future can be even better.

> Every successful man I have heard of has done the best he could with conditions as he found them, and not waited until the next year for better.
>
> E. W. HOWE, WRITER

If you're anything like me, though, high school was a difficult experience. Maybe you couldn't wait for graduation day to get here. Maybe you never made it into the "in crowd" and spent hours slaving over homework in order to maintain a C average. If that's how high school was for you, I want you to know that life doesn't have to stay that way. Things can be much, much better.

Anybody who has gone back to a high school reunion can tell you the same thing. Some of the people who were big stars in high school never quite make it in the "real world."

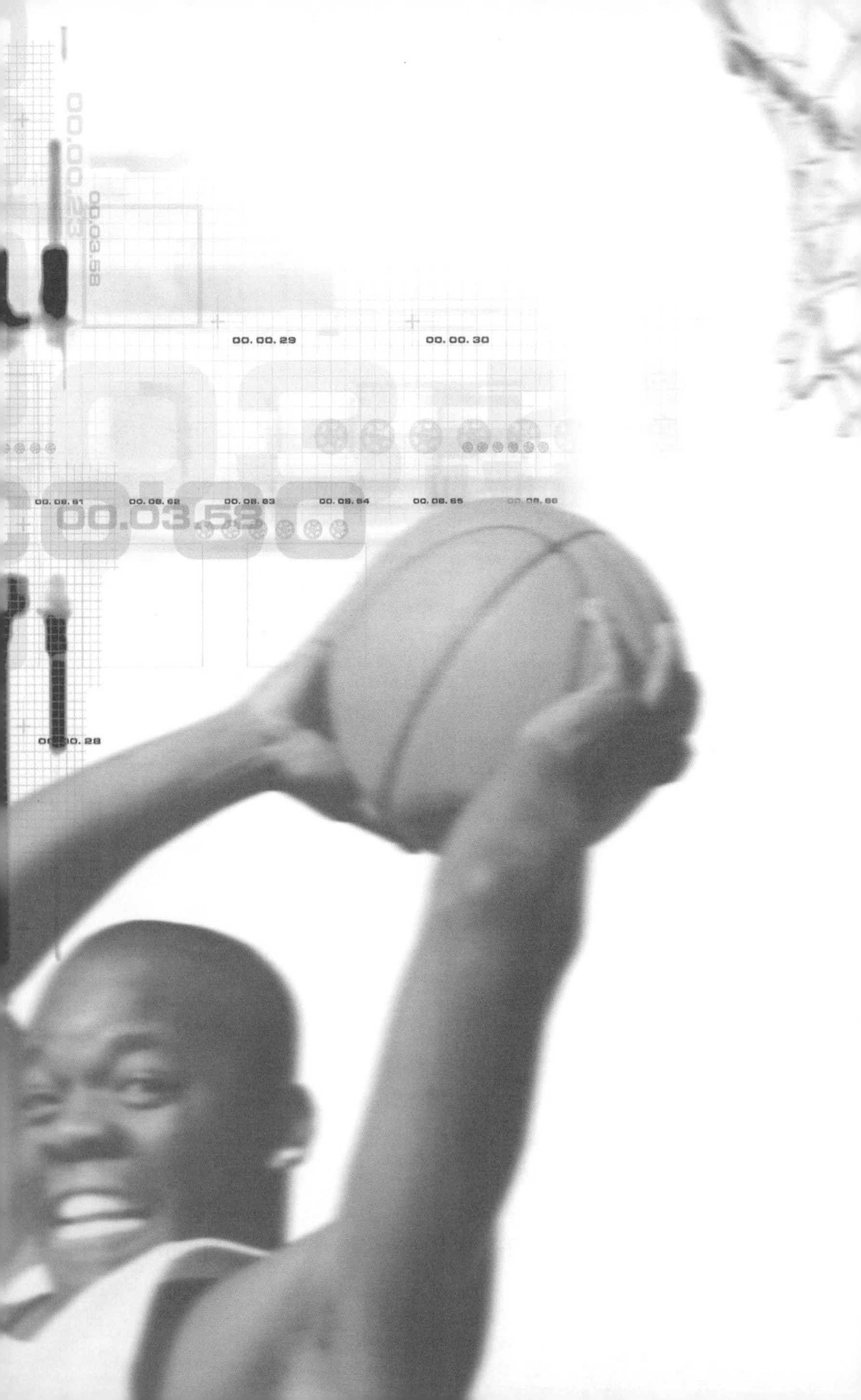

And some who couldn't seem to do anything right in high school go on to become successful, well-adjusted adults.

Let me tell you about a young man who was considered to be a dunce—a daydreamer who didn't pay attention in class and couldn't grasp the simplest concepts. People thought he'd never amount to anything.

But he proved their negative views wrong by working tirelessly to turn many of his daydreams into reality.

Perhaps you've heard of him. His name was Thomas Edison.

And maybe you've heard of another young man who was cut from his high school basketball team. He was kind of skinny, and his coach didn't think he was varsity material.

That's right. I talked about him in the introduction. His name is Michael Jordan, and he went on to become the greatest basketball player of all time.

History is full of similar examples of men and women who achieved success in life by overcoming tremendous odds.

For example, back in the 1930s an aspiring actress was told by a high-powered Hollywood executive that she didn't have what it took to make it in the entertainment business. He told her to go on back home and content herself with life as a housewife.

Now as far as I'm concerned, taking care of a family is just about the most important thing any woman can do. But this particular lady had a dream of making it in show business, and she wasn't about to let go of that dream.

Her name? Lucille Ball, the woman widely regarded as the top comedienne of the twentieth century. Nearly fifty years after leaving the air, her situation comedy *I Love Lucy* was ranked by *TV Guide* as the second-best television show of all time.

Think of all the laughter the world would've missed if Lucy had given up!

As these three examples prove, it doesn't really matter what other people say or think about you. God built you for success, not failure.

WHAT IS SUCCESS?

Mark Twain said, "Everyone talks about the weather, but nobody does anything about it." In our time, it may be true that everyone talks about success, but nobody really knows what it is.

I'm thinking of a young woman I met at Clemson University in South Carolina.

Everything was going her way. She had a perfect GPA. She was a star athlete. She was young, healthy, and attractive.

She should have been feeling on top of the world. But instead, she was uneasy, even frightened, about her future, and she didn't really know why.

I met this young woman while I was at Clemson talking to a group of students about a book I'd just written. I was signing books after my talk when I looked up into her fresh, earnest face.

"Mr. Williams, I really need to talk to you." She smiled, but there was desperation in her voice. "Can you give me a few minutes?" She looked back at the long line behind her. "I can wait until you're finished here."

"Sure," I said with a smile. I knew I had a couple of hours before I had to catch a flight to my next destination.

She waited patiently for a half hour or so until the crowd was gone. Then, as soon as the last book was signed, she was back.

"Now, what's on your mind?" I asked.

She told me her name was Maria and that she was from Yugoslavia. I was surprised, because she spoke excellent English, with only a hint of an accent. She had come to Clemson on a volleyball scholarship, and she had a 4.0 GPA. She was in the middle of her senior year and was having a great season on the volleyball court.

> **Don't aim for success. If you want it, just do what you love and believe in, and it will come naturally.**
>
> DAVID FROST, TV HOST

"I don't understand what's troubling you," I admitted.

She paused for a moment, seemingly searching for the right words to say. "Mr. Williams," she finally asked, "what's going to happen to me?"

Even though Maria didn't say so in so many words, I knew what she was thinking: *Is this all there is? I'm experiencing wonderful success. Everything's going my way. Life is good. I should be filled with joy, but instead I feel scared and empty.*

As I heard the frustration in her voice, my mind went back thirty-five years to Spartanburg, South Carolina, where the Philadelphia Phillies had just hired me to run their minor league baseball affiliate. I had always believed that if I set high goals for myself and then did everything I could to reach those goals, I would find true peace and contentment.

Failure is the condiment that gives success its flavor.

TRUMAN CAPOTE, AUTHOR

But that wasn't what happened.

Instead I discovered that the more material success I had, the more frustrated I became. I felt like I was chasing the Great American Dream, which always lay just out of my reach.

Why was I feeling that way? Because I was pursuing the wrong goals. I had lost focus of what was really important.

Too often we put a high value on things that aren't worth much, while things with true worth are overlooked and disregarded. As a result, we fight and claw to become "king of the hill," thinking that when we get to the summit, we will find success and happiness. Instead, we often find disappointment, because such types of "success" are easily lost.

I have known many athletes who were miserable and unhappy despite multimillion-dollar contracts and worldwide fame and adulation. They had everything fortune and fame could bring, but something was missing—and they didn't know what it was.

Money is important, but it's not the key to personal success. Fame cannot satisfy the need for a meaningful life. Neither can power . . . or pleasure.

And in the same way, failure cannot keep you from being successful in the long run.

Building Success from Failure

A newspaper reporter once asked a tight-lipped bank president, "What's the secret of your success?"

"Two words," the banker answered.

"And what would they be?"

"Right decisions."

"And how do you make the right decisions?" the reporter persisted.

"Experience."

"And how do you get experience?"

"Two words," came the familiar answer.

"And what are they?"

"Wrong decisions."

Like that banker, I've made my share of wrong decisions, but that's okay. Sometimes in order to find the right answer to a problem, it is necessary to discover and discard the wrong answer.

For example, Thomas Edison failed one thousand times in his quest to invent the electric lightbulb. When asked if so many failures didn't make him feel like giving up, Edison said no—because every time a "wrong way" was eliminated, he knew he was one step closer to discovering the only "right way" to make his invention work.

Similarly, in life, there are many roads that seem to lead to success, but which instead lead to disappointment and failure. In the pages ahead, we'll explore each of these roads and discover how to keep moving along toward true success.

TWO

FORTUNE

Money Can Buy You (Almost) Everything

Money has never made a man happy yet, nor will it. There is nothing in its nature to produce Happiness.

Benjamin Franklin

I DON'T CARE TOO MUCH FOR MONEY. Money can't buy me love."

Easy enough for the Beatles to say. After all, while they were topping the charts with that song, millions of dollars in royalties were pouring into their bank accounts.

Maybe money can't buy you love. But it can buy you plenty of other things. In fact, it's almost impossible to get by without money. Everyone needs it.

Lisa Bonet is a talented young actress who became famous—and rich—as a teenager, due to her role on the top-ranked 1980s sitcom *The Cosby Show*. Musing over her fame and fortune, she said, "We're taught that success is money, or being famous, or holding a high position. And for someone like me, or other young actors who achieve that so early, it's like, 'Where do you go from here if this is it?'"

The truth is that money *isn't* it. There's much more to life.

I heard a story about a successful businessman who was visiting a small coastal village. While there, he saw a small boat dock at the pier. Inside the boat was just one fisherman and several large yellowfin tuna.

"How long did it take you to catch these fish?" the businessman asked.

"Only a little while," the fisherman answered.

"Well, why didn't you stay out longer and catch more fish?"

"Because I have enough to take care of my family," the fisherman replied.

The businessman looked confused. "But what will you do with the rest of your day?"

"I'll take a nap. Play with my children. Enjoy being with my wife."

The businessman shook his head. "Listen, I could help you set up a successful business here."

"Really?" the fisherman asked. "How?"

"First, you'd have to spend more time fishing so you could sell enough fish to buy a bigger boat. Eventually you'd buy several boats—a whole fleet of them. The next step would be to open a cannery so you could control the processing and distribution of your product. Eventually, of course, you'd have to move to Los Angeles or New York to run your business, which would be spread all over the world."

The fisherman wasn't convinced. "How long would all this take?" he asked.

"Twenty years or so."

"And then what?"

The businessman was growing impatient. "You'd sell your company and make millions."

"And after that?"

"You'd retire, of course."

"And then?"

"You'd move to a small coastal fishing village where you could take naps during the day, play with your grandkids, enjoy time with your wife . . ."

You see, some people don't recognize success even when they are nose to nose with it!

If you've ever been tempted to believe that money and success are the same thing, consider this. In 1923, several of the world's wealthiest men gathered for an important meeting at Chicago's Edgewater Hotel. Twenty-five years later, a reporter checked up on what had happened to these men. Here's what he discovered:

Samuel Insull died broke in a foreign country, a fugitive from justice

Howard Hopson was confined to a mental hospital

Arthur Cutten died broke

Richard Whitney was in prison

Albert Fall had his prison sentence commuted so he could die at home

Jesse Livermore committed suicide

Ivar Krueger also took his own life

Leon Fraser was yet another suicide

All of these men knew how to make money. But none of them can be called a success. As Billy Graham once said, "There is nothing wrong with men possessing riches. The wrong comes when riches possess men."

The Bible says that the love of money is the root of all evil, and I have seen this to be true. Whereas money can bring about tremendous good if used properly, the love of money can separate friends, cause one person to treat another person in a brutal and shameful way, and produce all sorts of criminal behavior.

However you look at it, the pursuit of money is the first detour on the road to true success. Money is important, but it's not *that* important.

"But how can I determine what's important?" you might ask. Well, here are five truths about money that everyone should know:

1. WHERE MONEY IS CONCERNED, SLOW AND STEADY WINS THE RACE.

There are people who win the lottery and get rich overnight. But they're very rare. In fact, I've never met one. Also rare are the people who come up with one big idea and make zillions of dollars in a matter of days. I haven't met many of those folks either.

When my son Jimmy was in the eighth grade, his life was changed because of a speech given by financial consultant Jim Seneff. Jim spoke at my son's school because his son, Tim, was a student there.

Jim told the young people that if they wanted to be financially successful, they should spend only what was necessary when they were in their twenties. Everything else should be invested and allowed to grow over time.

Jimmy took that to heart, and today, at age twenty-eight, he is a wealthy young man. And he has done this through saving, wise investing, and the miracle of compound interest.

Financial expert Brian Tracy says that a person who invests 100 dollars a month between the ages of 21 and 65, and who earns a compounded interest rate of 10 percent, would be able to retire with a net worth of just over 1.1 million dollars.

If you want to figure out how long it will take your money to double, Tracy says, simply divide the interest rate into 72. For example, if you are receiving a 6 percent return, divide 6 into 72 and you'll come up with 12. That means it will take 12 years for your money to double.

I've known some star athletes with multimillion-dollar contracts who could not live within their means. The more they made, the more they spent, forever teetering on the edge of financial disaster. On the other hand, I've known folks who were able to live comfortably on a small fraction of what those athletes made.

How did they do it? Simple.

- They lived within their means.
- They made it a point to save part of what they made.

Larry Bird, the Hall of Famer who led the Boston Celtics for so many years, has always been one of my favorite people. I loved Larry's skill and intensity as a player and then as a coach of the Indiana Pacers. And I appreciated his levelheaded attitude about life. He was a superstar who didn't act the part. Even when he was making millions of dollars every year, he didn't act like it. "I've always been careful to save my money," he says. He and his wife, Dinah, bought a $100,000 house. It was nice, but it wasn't a palace. He says, "We didn't run out and spend all our money, because we knew there would be a time when it was over."

He remembers that some of his teammates thought he was crazy. "Some of the guys who made far less than me bought the $700,000 homes and the Rolex watches and the big luxury cars. I used to tell them, 'You're crazy. You should be saving your money.' They'd just laugh and make jokes about me stashing my money away, but I could see what they were doing. They were throwing away their future."

He continues, "By the time they realized what I was telling them was true, it was too late. I can't tell you how many ex-teammates have asked me for money. It's heartbreaking for me to say no, but I do, because I warned them. I told them to save."

No matter how much money you make, get in the habit of saving some of it. Mark Twain said that "nobody ever went broke saving money," and it's true. As the Bible says, "He who gathers money little by little makes it grow" (Prov. 13:11).

Include saving as part of your monthly budget and put the power of compound interest to work. The results just may amaze you!

2. MONEY IS OFTEN A BY-PRODUCT OF PERSONAL ACHIEVEMENT.

If you took a poll of the richest people in the world, I'm sure you'd discover that the vast majority of them did not set out with the idea of making money. Instead you'd find that they were passionately interested in an idea, a business, or a dream of some kind. I'm certain most of them would agree with financier Warren Buffett, who says, "Money is a by-product of doing something I like doing extremely well."

I enjoy speaking to groups of high school and college students because I love their energy and enthusiasm and their penchant for asking difficult questions. One of those questions often is, "How do I know what to do with my life?"

And my answer is, "Figure out as early as you possibly can what you love to do, and then find a way to get paid for it."

I was seven years old when my dad took me to my first major league baseball game at Philadelphia's Shibe Park. (I won't tell you the year, but it was a long time ago.) I loved everything about that experience—the sights, the sounds, the smells, the excitement of the game. I knew then that I wanted to spend my life in professional sports. And that's what I've done. You know what? I would have done it all for free! But don't tell the owners. With nineteen children, I have an awful lot of bills to pay!

> Compound interest is considered one of the great miracles of all of human history and economics. Albert Einstein described it as the most powerful force in our society. When you let money accumulate at compound interest over a long enough period of time, it increases more than you can imagine.
>
> BRIAN TRACY,
> FINANCIAL EXPERT

Remember that money won't come to you simply because you have a desire for it. It will come, instead, because you work hard, or because you provide a service that other people are willing to pay for, or because you devote yourself to making the world a better place.

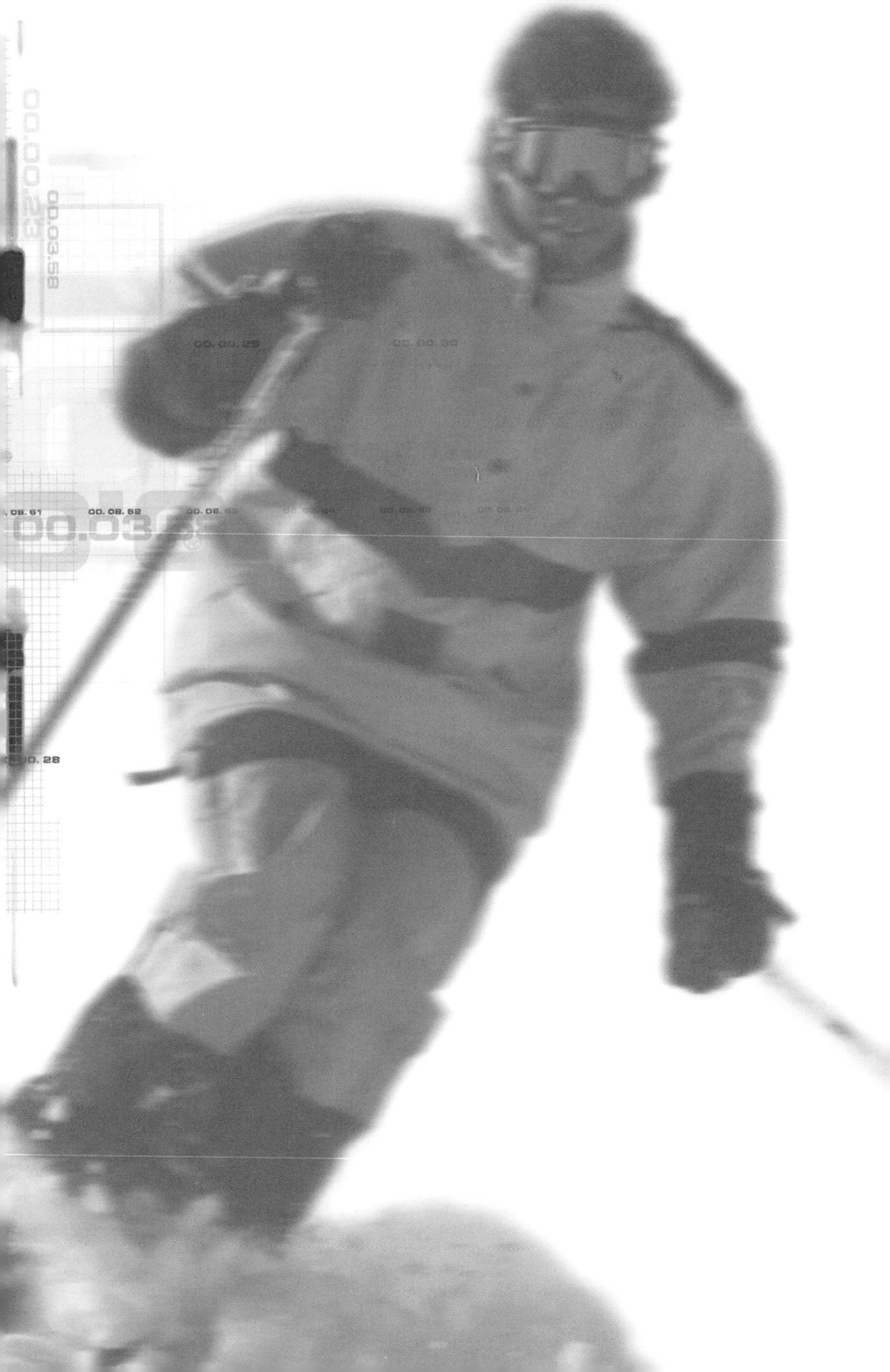

But don't just take my word for it. Here's what some wealthy people have had to say about the pursuit of riches:

Harvey Firestone said, "If you ask yourself why you are in business and can find no answer other than, 'I want to make money,' you will save money by getting out of business and going to work for someone. . . . for you are in business without sufficient reason."

Steven Spielberg said, "I'm not really interested in making money; that's always come as the result of success."

Bill Gates said that if he had to choose between his job and having great wealth, "I'd choose my job. It's a much bigger thrill to lead a team of thousands of talented, bright people than it is to have a big bank account."

Oprah Winfrey said something very similar: "I would do what I'm doing even if I weren't getting paid."

Remember, the pursuit of money often leads nowhere. The pursuit of personal excellence and achievement is more likely to produce a full bank account.

3. IF MONEY IS WHAT YOU REALLY WANT, YOU'LL NEVER GET ENOUGH.

Listen to Chuck Colson, founder of Prison Fellowship:

Practicing the religion of consumerism is like drinking salt water. The more you drink, the thirstier you get. There is never enough wealth and power to satisfy; never enough material possessions to blot out guilt, and no matter how pleasant or attractive such things can make our brief existence here on earth, they cannot carry us beyond. For the old adage is apt: "You can't take it with you."

An economist by the name of H. F. Clark undertook a study in which he determined that no matter how much money people make, they want about 25 percent more. In other words, the man who makes $40,000 a year thinks he'd be happy if only he had a salary of $50,000. But the woman who earns $50,000 thinks she needs about $62,500, and so on.

Clark's research shows that the more money people make, the more they spend and thus, the more they need. His conclusion? More money doesn't really satisfy anyone. It just increases the appetite for more.

Listen to what David Robinson of the NBA's San Antonio Spurs said:

> Probably the most challenging thing I face is the money aspect of my life. . . . The key for me is learning to draw the line between possessing things and things possessing me. I want to keep my heart pure for the Lord, and there's a lot of things money can do to distract me.

Yes, money can distract a person from what's really important. In his story *How Much Land Does a Man Need?* Leo Tolstoy tells of a Russian peasant named Pakhom who is convinced that he will be happy only when he owns as much land as a very wealthy nobleman. Therefore he is overjoyed when someone offers to give him as much land as he can circle on foot from dawn to dusk of one day.

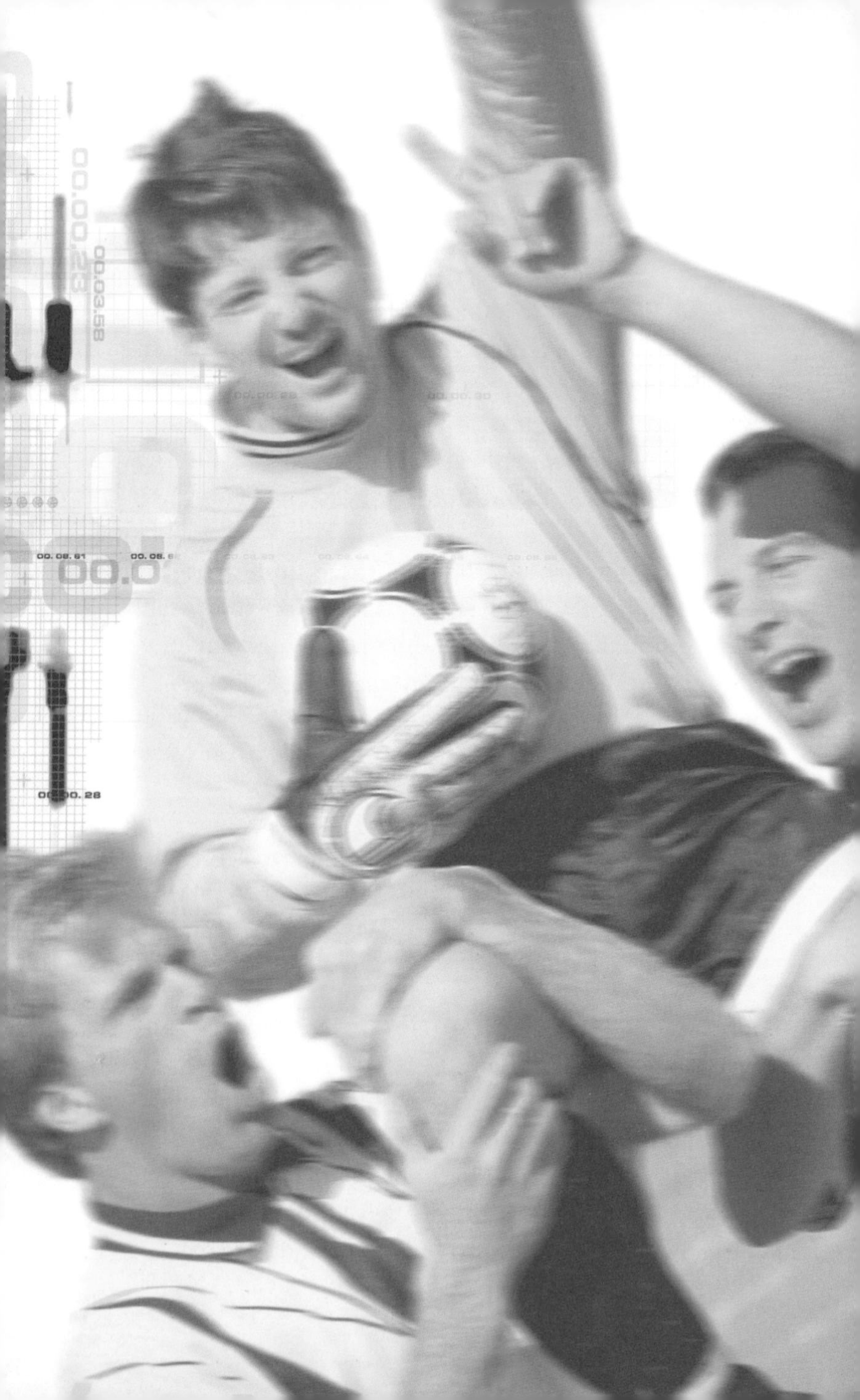

When the sun first comes over the horizon on this all-important day, Pakhom takes off as fast as he can go. The sun beats down, but he will not stop. His muscles ache and burn, but he keeps on running without stopping to eat, drink, or rest. Just before sunset, the peasant staggers back to his starting place.

He made it! He's rich beyond his wildest dreams! But as he takes his final step, he crumples to the ground—dead. Now the only land he needs lies six feet beneath the ground.

> The man who starts out with the idea of getting rich won't succeed. You must have a larger ambition.
>
> JOHN D. ROCKEFELLER

Too late, Pakhom learned the truth that Franklin D. Roosevelt taught: "Happiness lies not in the possession of money [or land]. It lies in the joy of achievement; in the thrill of creative effort."

4. MONEY IS IMPORTANT, BUT THERE ARE MANY THINGS MORE IMPORTANT.

Some people define themselves by how much money or how many expensive "goodies" they've been able to accumulate. But what a shallow means of measuring the value of human life!

As writer Linda Henley says, "So many of us define ourselves by what we have, what we wear, what kind of house we live in, and what kind of car we drive. If you think of yourself as the woman with the Cartier watch and the Hermes scarf, a house fire will destroy not only your possessions, but yourself."

Not too long ago, I read an interview with a wealthy man in his midseventies who had amassed a fortune estimated at more than $750 million. When the interviewer asked him if he had any regrets, the fellow replied, "Yes. I wanted to be worth at least a billion dollars by the time I died . . . but I don't think I'm going to make it."

What a pity a man could live so long without realizing that money is only important because of the good things you can do with it. Far too many people have made the tragic mistake of giving up things that are far more important than money in order to get money.

Health is more important than money, so don't ruin it by working one hundred hours a week trying to get rich. Money won't buy your health back after you ruin it.

Friendship is more important than money, so don't turn your back on your friends to spend your time chasing wealth. Money won't make you happy if you wind up all by yourself. I recently read about three women who have been best friends since they met as Campfire Girls more than sixty years ago! As one of the friends says, "Old friends see each other as they really are. You have that special feeling, you understand each other so much better because you've had the same experiences, teachers, goals." How could anyone put a money value on a relationship like that?

Your family is more important than money. In 1951, Lillian Vernon placed a $500 ad in *Seventeen* magazine, offering to sell monogrammed leather purses and matching belts. She used the $2,000 she had received as a wedding gift to purchase those purses and belts and monogrammed them at her kitchen table. From that small beginning, she grew a company that does $235 million worth of business every year, with a catalog circulation of more than 141 million. When Mrs. Vernon was asked for her 10 tips of business success, her number one was "Make time for yourself and your family." Making time for your family is that important. You'd have to be pretty stupid to trade your family for money, yet this is exactly what some people do.

Love is more important than money. And remember, the Beatles were telling the truth when they said "Money can't buy me love."

Self-respect is more important than money. I'm constantly amazed by the things people will do to get money. I was channel surfing a few days ago when a game show captured my attention for a few minutes. Contestants were asked to do things like eat a handful of bugs for a huge amount of money. And everybody I saw was willing to try it! It made me think of a quote by W. K. Kellogg, CEO of Kellogg cereals. "Dollars have never been known to produce character, and character will never be produced by money." If you have to choose between self-respect—or character—and money, choose self-respect. It will pay off in the long run!

God is more important than money. The Bible has quite a bit to say about those who put money first in their lives. It tells us that no man can serve God and money at the same time. It tells us that the love of money is the root of all kinds of evil. It tells us that it is easier for a camel to pass through the eye of a needle than for a rich man to enter heaven. And it warns us that we are not to love "the world, neither the things that are in the world" (1 John 2:15 KJV). Of course, nowhere in the Bible does it say that money in and of itself is evil. The problem arises when money and material possessions take the place that should be reserved for God and God alone. "Neon" Deion Sanders says he has finally learned that money and possessions cannot bring happiness. That comes, he says, only from the peace of God. "And, you know, that's free. It doesn't cost you anything."

Comedian Richard Pryor, who was critically burned in an accident, would agree that money isn't the most important thing in life. He once told Johnny Carson that when he was sick, "All I could think of was to call on God. I didn't call the Bank of America once."

5. GOD LOVES A CHEERFUL GIVER.

That's what the Bible says. And because it's true, I believe that cheerful givers are blessed in important ways. For instance, psychiatrist Karl Menninger says he has found that "generous people are very rarely mentally ill people." He says that "money-giving" seems to be a very good means for measuring a person's mental health.

I agree with Francis Bacon, who said that money is like fertilizer—not good unless spread. Diedre Pujols, wife of the St. Louis Cardinals's Albert Pujols, would agree as well. She says that she and her husband try to give "willingly and lovingly," as God tells them to do. "Albert and I understand that the money he makes during our lifetime is not our money. We're very committed and excited to give, and to see what God is going to do for us next."

Muhammad Ali says that he never understood the joy money can bring until he began to give it away. Two of the richest men of the last century, John D. Rockefeller and Andrew Carnegie, said the same thing. So if you want to be a success in life, I suggest that you learn the same art these three men learned—the art of being a cheerful giver. Don't say, "Someday when I'm rich, I'm going to give away lots of money." Start now, with whatever you have. Give some money to a missions organization, sponsor a child through an organization like World Vision or Compassion, make a donation to a local rescue mission. In doing so, I believe you'll discover the blessings that God imparts to those who are willing to give a portion of what they have.

I want to conclude this chapter with a story about the late Pete Maravich. As general manager of the Atlanta Hawks, I traded Maravich to the New Orleans Jazz (now the Utah Jazz) on May 3, 1974. I remember the date because it was my birthday. After the trade was completed, I drove out to Maravich's apartment to give him the news. I thought he might welcome the trade, since he had played college basketball at Louisiana State.

When I told him he'd been traded, all he asked was, "What did you get for me?"

I told him, and it was a lot, including a couple of top-round draft picks. He shook his head as if I'd made the dumbest deal in NBA history. "Is that all?" he asked.

Later on, I was thrilled to see Pete give his life to Christ and become an incredible force in God's kingdom. And I love this quote from Pistol Pete: "Money will buy you everything but happiness. It will pay your fare to everywhere but heaven. If you seek happiness and pleasure, you will never find it—ever. If you have the wisdom to seek Jesus Christ, pleasure will find you."

Obviously, then, money is *not* what life is all about.

THREE

FAME

I Know You! You're What's-His-Name!

The sound of a great name dies like an echo; the splendor of fame fades into nothing; but the grace of a fine spirit pervades the places through which it has passed.

JAMES THURBER, AUTHOR

WHAT, ME FAMOUS?

Not exactly.

But then again, I do give a lot of speeches every year, I've written quite a few books, and I'm often invited to appear on TV. So sometimes I get recognized.

For instance, I'll be eating in a restaurant when someone walks by and does a double take. Or I'll see someone at a neighboring table staring at me. They know I'm "somebody." But they're not sure who.

Sometimes, it's flattering. But more often, it's embarrassing. I've even had people come up and point at me.

"Hey, I know you! You're . . ."

And then they stand there, waiting for me to tell them who I am.

"I'm Pat Williams," I say with a smile.

"Pat Williams? No, that's not it! You're . . . you're . . . what's-his-name!"

No, "fame" isn't all it's cracked up to be. If you want further evidence, try this quicky quiz.

Name all the members of the Spice Girls.

Can't do it? How about just one of them?

If you can do even that, you have a much better memory than most people. Like many pop stars, the Spice Girls had a short career and then faded into obscurity. But just a few years ago, almost every teenager from Bangor to Banning could have told me the names of all the members of that group. But that was then. This is now.

And you know what? I'm willing to bet that today's superstars—like *NSYNC and the Backstreet Boys—will also be forgotten five or ten years from now.

Sad, but true—most fame is fleeting.

A few years ago, two days after the Academy Awards were presented, the *National Enquirer* asked one hundred people if they could name the winners of the Best Picture, Best Actor, and Best Actress awards. Only one in four got it right. Not only that, but forty-four out of the one hundred couldn't name even one of the three!

The Academy Awards ceremony had been televised live and seen by over sixty-five million people. Following that, the winners' names and faces had been seen on newspapers and news shows throughout the country. But still, as the *Enquirer* poll shows, most people had already forgotten who the winners were.

For most, fame passes quickly. Fifty years ago, the newspaper *The Observer* had this to say about British Prime Minister Winston Churchill: "In a thousand years from now, his name will be popularly known; it will conjure up a warm glow, a proud smile and signify what is most bold and generous in human nature."

Oh, really? Today, one-third of all British schoolchildren have never heard of Churchill. Of those who have, some believe he was an American president, while others guess that he must have been a songwriter. So much for popularity that lasts a thousand years!

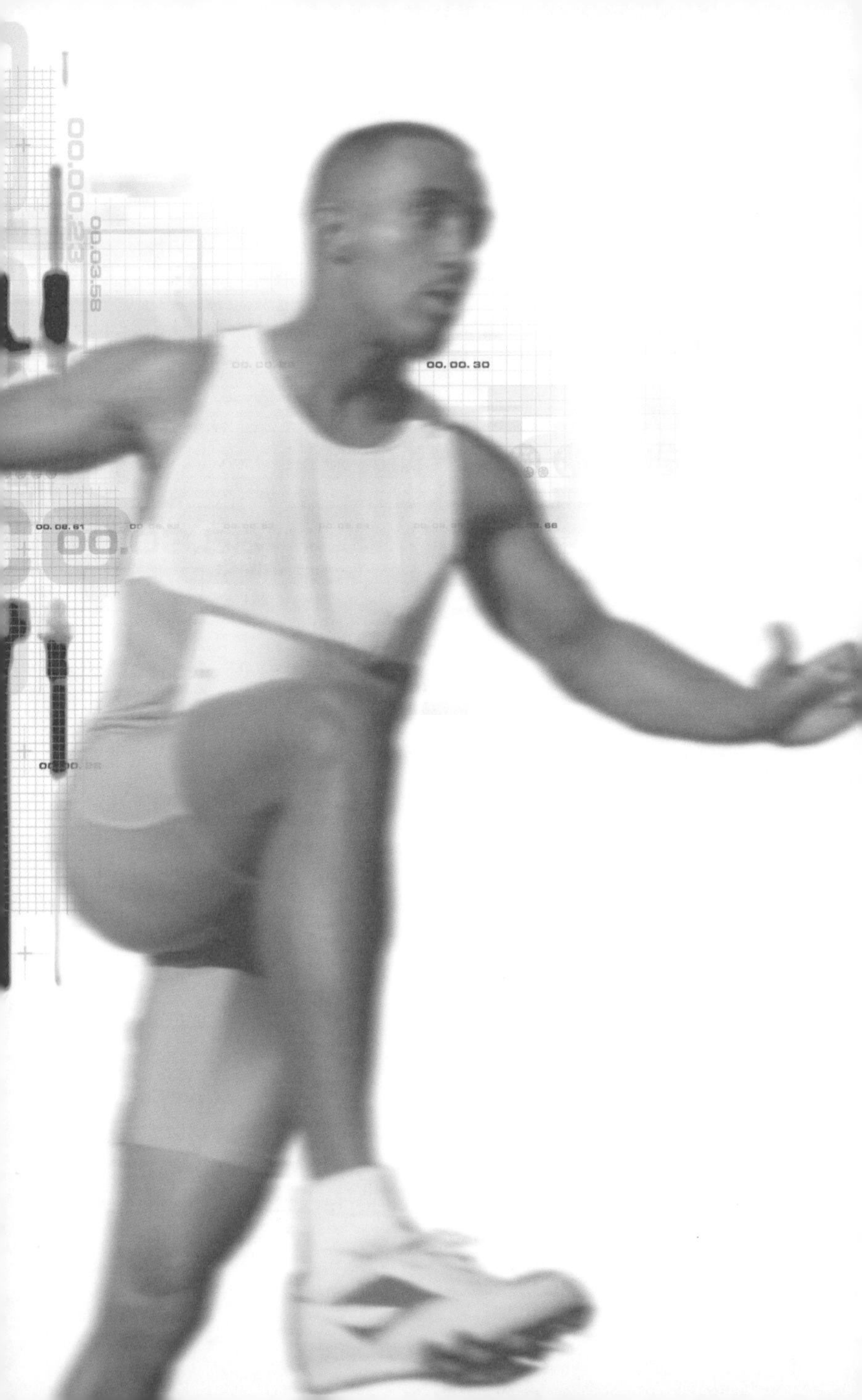

I realize it's natural to want people to know who you are. The desire to be popular is an integral part of human nature. And there are many benefits that can come from having people know who you are. Madonna said, "The best thing about fame is that I never have to wait for a table at a restaurant." But I can think of many other reasons why fame can be a good thing. Here are just a few of them.

1. FAME MAKES PEOPLE WANT TO HEAR WHAT YOU HAVE TO SAY.

Fame can give you an opportunity to speak out on important issues. For example, in my hometown of Orlando, there's a rescue mission that does a great job of getting homeless men off the streets and helping them become contributing members of society. If an "ordinary Joe" made a commercial for the mission and said, "This is a great place. I hope you'll make a contribution," most people wouldn't pay much attention. But if Grant Hill or one of the Orlando Magic's other star players made that message, you can bet people would sit up and take notice and—hopefully—send a check to the mission! Right or wrong, fame gets people's attention.

2. FAME CAN MAKE YOU MORE ACCOUNTABLE.

Fame can provide you with the opportunity to be a role model. Several years ago, a fellow by the name of Gary

Hart wanted to be President of the United States. When rumors he was having an extramarital affair surfaced, he denied the stories and basically issued a challenge to the reporters covering his campaign: "I dare you to catch me." They did. Gary Hart's presidential hopes were dashed. In our information-hungry society, it seems that celebrities can't get away with anything. Bill Clinton found this out. So did Jim Bakker and Jimmy Swaggart, and . . . well, the list could go on and on. Col. Harland Sanders founded the Kentucky Fried Chicken restaurant chain and as a result became world famous. He was once asked about what it was like to have one of the most recognized faces in the world, and he replied, "You don't mind being known if you're behaving yourself." If you're famous in this society, and if you want people to continue to like and respect you, you'd better stay on your toes—all the time!

3. FAME OPENS DOORS.

Fame can get you places. But whether this is a good thing or a bad thing depends on the places you want to go. Yes, being famous can open doors to the best seats at the theater, at fancy restaurants, at sporting events, and so on. But it can also open more important doors, like getting you an audience with influential men and women who are shaping public policy. Very few doors are closed to the celebrities among us.

But although fame can be a good thing, it has many drawbacks as well. Let's look at just three of them.

1. FAME CANNOT BRING INNER PEACE.

The late George Harrison once was asked what his life was like when the Beatles were at the height of their popularity. Certainly, his interviewer expected him to talk about how much fun he had and how great it was to have nearly everyone in the world know his name. But that's not what he said.

"Being a Beatle was a nightmare, a horror story," Harrison responded. "I don't even want to think about it."

Why not?

"At first we all thought we wanted the fame and that. After a bit, we realized that fame wasn't really what we were after at all, just the fruits of it."

In a sense, fame held the Beatles captive. And when it did, Harrison said, "I, for one, became depressed. Is this all we have to look forward to in life? Being chased around by a crowd of hooting lunatics from one . . . hotel room to the next? How stupid it all is. All that big hassle to make it, only to end up as performing fleas."

Everyone called Elvis "The King." He sold over one hundred million records, starred in dozens of movies, and was hailed by adoring fans everywhere he went. But in 1976, Elvis told a reporter, "I'm so tired of being Elvis Presley."

More than thirty years after his death, Jimi Hendrix is still regarded as one of the greatest rock guitarists of all time. His career was reaching its peak just as the Beatles were going their separate ways. At the end of a concert in 1970, Hendrix smashed his guitar onto the stage floor while the audience applauded and screamed. He then fell to his knees and stayed that way, kneeling motionless in the spotlight for several minutes. The applause stopped as the auditorium became enveloped in concerned silence. Was something wrong with Jimi Hendrix?

Finally, he spoke softly. "If you know real peace, I want to visit with you backstage."

Then he walked away, leaving the splintered pieces of his guitar scattered on the stage behind him.

Apparently, nobody responded to Hendrix's unusual invitation. Several days later, still in his twenties, Jimi Hendrix died of a drug overdose.

Fame wasn't enough for him. Or Kurt Cobain. Or Marilyn Monroe. Or Janis Joplin. Or any one of dozens of other famous people I could name who came to a tragic end—who learned too late that fame and adulation are not enough to bring peace of mind and spirit.

As Atlanta Braves slugger Chipper Jones said, "Being famous is not all it's cracked up to be. . . . You have to spend a lot of time away from home. You have to miss a lot of firsts—first steps, first words."

2. FAME CAN CHANGE YOU—FOR THE WORSE.

Jesus said it is easier for a camel to pass through the eye of a needle than for a rich man to enter God's kingdom. I think it must be even harder to get into heaven if you're famous. That's because fame changes you.

One of the problems with being famous is that you tend to believe your own press releases and fan mail. In other words, fame distorts your perspective on who you really are. I don't want to name any names, but I've seen guys' personalities change completely after tasting success in the NBA. When they first come into the league, they're nice, polite kids who say things like "thank you" and "please" and "sir." But after a few minutes in the spotlight, their attitude becomes "If you have something to say to me, tell my agent about it" and "I demand more playing time."

I've seen players who were loaded with talent mess up their careers because they began to think they were more important than the team. They started skipping team meetings and showing up late for practice, and pretty soon, there wasn't a team in the NBA that wanted them, no matter how much talent they had.

They should've listened to the words of legendary college basketball coach John Wooden, who said, "Talent is God-given; be humble. Fame is man-given; be thankful. Conceit is self-given; be careful."

Or if they didn't want to hear wisdom from a man of Coach's stature, they could've listened to Dennis Rodman, who said,

> This pro ball business is nothing but a fantasy, that's all it is. It's like going to Fantasy Island and fulfilling all your dreams. But once you get out, it's like you're still living a dream but you don't have the applause, you don't have the cheers. All that is gone and everything is suddenly silent. Nobody knows who you are—you're a has-been. All the people can do is say, "Remember, remember he made that great move fifteen years ago."

I'm happy to tell you of one person who doesn't seem to be in danger of letting fame go to her head: Sarah Hughes. Sarah is the young lady who at age sixteen won the gold medal for figure skating at the 2002 Winter Olympics. Young Sarah went from being an anonymous high school junior to someone who is known—and adored—by millions of people all over the world. Her dazzling performance was thrilling for all Americans, giving us something to feel good about in the wake of September 11.

After a triumph like that, it would be easy for a girl like Sarah to develop an attitude, demand special treatment, and think she's better than other people. But from what I've heard, she's back in school, studying algebra and conducting herself like a "normal" person. And if that's true, I think her return to ordinary life represents just as great a triumph as the one she pulled off in Salt Lake City. She's setting an example we'd all do well to follow.

Another way fame changes people for the worse is by introducing them to a wide variety of self-destructive temptations. When you're famous, people want to do things for you. You want drugs? You got them. Casual sex? There are plenty of beautiful people anxious and willing to sleep with you if you're a celebrity. Alcohol? Lots of people anxious to buy you a drink.

But this kind of life is not a paradise. All too often it becomes a hell from which there is no escape. Sadly, fame corrupts even men and women who have devoted their lives to serving God. And there's nothing new about this. The Bible tells us that when Saul was chosen to be king of Israel, he was so shy that he hid, apparently hoping the crown would be passed to someone else. But just a few years later, he was totally full of himself. So much so that when the people of Israel applauded David for his victory over Goliath, Saul immediately began plotting to kill David.

In his story *The Great Divorce*, C. S. Lewis writes about a celebration in heaven. Thousands of people have come from all over paradise to honor a great hero from earth's history. The main character in the book, a newcomer to heaven, manages to work his way to the front of the line because he wants to see who has stirred up so much excitement and interest.

He's surprised when a rather ordinary-looking older woman passes by. She doesn't look the least bit like a celebrity. He can't recall having seen her face before. Her name doesn't mean a thing to him. But he's told that because of her many acts of unselfish service for God's kingdom, this unassuming lady is a hero in the eyes of God, and thus in the eyes of all those living in heaven.

The point of the story is that the things that make a person popular here on earth are not necessarily the same things that make a person popular with God.

I don't know about you, but I'd choose the praise of God over the praise of people any day!

3. FAME CAN MAKE YOU MISERABLE.

Fame isn't all it's cracked up to be. In fact, it can make you miserable. Let's hear what some famous people have had to say about fame.

> **Frank Sinatra:** "It [fame] just changes everything. You can't go to a beach. You can't walk into a movie. You can't stand on a corner and eat a hot dog. You want the fame, but baby, you pay a price."

Madonna: "Finally you get what you've been searching for all those years, and then you spend the rest of your life trying to hide."

Bette Midler: "I always wanted to be a big star, even before I knew what being a big star meant."

Dennis Weaver: "So many people in Hollywood are desperate for inner fulfillment. They chase false ideas of happiness and still feel discontent. They feel hollow and empty inside despite their fame, their big paychecks, their limos, and their jewels."

Oprah Winfrey: "For me, greatness isn't determined by fame. I don't know if you want to go to the bathroom and have people say, 'Is that you in there? What are you doing?' That is the price of fame—and then reading about it in the tabloids. I don't know if you want that for yourselves, but I do believe that what you want is a sense of greatness. Dr. [Martin Luther] King says that greatness is determined by service."

The consensus, then, is that being famous does not ensure success in life.

What about being powerful? Maybe that's the key.

FOUR

POWER

I'M AT THE TOP—NOW WHAT?

*Nearly all men can stand adversity,
but if you want to test a man's character, give him power.*

ABRAHAM LINCOLN

SO FAR, WE'VE SEEN that true success doesn't consist of having wealth or fame. And now we come to another place where men and women often seek success in life, and that is . . . power.

I believe that, like money and fame, power can be either good or bad. After all, power is a necessary thing.

For example, I'm grateful that when terrorists struck a blow against the United States on September 11, 2001, our government had men and women in power who were ready, willing, and able to strike back in order to protect our country from terror.

And there are many other situations in our society where the use of power is an absolute necessity. Frankly, there are many types of power I'm glad I don't have!

- I wouldn't want to be the judge who sentences dangerous criminals to spend the rest of their lives in prison. But I'm grateful for judges who have that power and are willing to use it.

- I wouldn't want to be the captain of a battalion of firefighters going up against a three-alarm fire. But I'm grateful for people who are willing to handle that kind of power.

- I wouldn't want to be the brain surgeon responsible for such delicate surgery, in which one small slip could cripple or kill someone. But I'm grateful that brain surgeons have the skill and power necessary to save human lives.

So am I afraid of power in general? Not at all! There are types of power I'm quite comfortable with. For example, when it comes to the power needed to run a sports franchise, hey, I'm your man! It's a tough job, yes. But it doesn't scare me!

QUENCHING THE THIRST FOR POWER

So far, all the power we've talked about is necessary and good. Judges need power or criminals would just laugh at them. Firefighter captains need power or there'd be a lot of houses lost to fires. Surgeons need the power of knowledge and skill or they wouldn't be able to save lives. And people who run sports franchises or other businesses need power to make and enforce important decisions or their businesses would crumble.

But some pursue power for power's sake. They want to get to the point where they can yell "Jump!" and have people ask "How high?" Chuck Colson, founder of Prison Fellowship, quotes Plato, who said, "He who seeks power is not fit to hold it." In other words, if power comes to you, let it come as a result of what you have achieved, not simply because you spent your life chasing after it!

So the first thing everyone needs to know about power is that it should never be pursued for its own sake.

The second thing everyone needs to know is that there are many people who *do* pursue power for its own sake, and it's good to be on the lookout for them. They can cause lots of trouble.

I'm sure you've heard this old saying: "Power corrupts, and absolute power corrupts absolutely." Over the last century, the truth of this phrase has been borne out again and again. In the developing world, many well-meaning men have fought to topple corrupt regimes, promising that once they were in power, they would work to build a just society. But once they gained power, most of them forgot all about justice and freedom and became even more corrupt than the regimes they sought to replace.

> Contrary to what some people think, sharing power increases your power. . . . The more you empower others, the bigger you become in their eyes. There is a law in the universe which says that power shared returns. Power withheld diminishes.
>
> SHEILA MURRAY BETHEL,
> AUTHOR

Anne Frank, a Jewish girl who died in a Nazi concentration camp at the age of fifteen, saw power at its very worst. Her diary was recovered after the war and became the source of a best-selling book and an acclaimed movie. In her diary, she wrote, "Human worth does not lie in the riches or power, but in character or goodness."

Anne Frank was only a child when she died. Yet she was wiser by far than those who took her life. She was an innocent victim of power gone mad. And there have been many thousands just like her, because this thirst for power is nothing new. During the Revolutionary War, John Adams had this to say about American officers:

> They worry one another, like Mastiffs, scrambling for rank and pay like apes for nuts. I believe there is not one principle which predominates in human nature, so much in every stage of life, from the cradle to the grave, in males and females, old and young, black and white, rich and poor, high and low, as this passion for superiority.

Here are some other important truths about power:

1. POWER IS STRENGTHENED, NOT WEAKENED, WHEN YOU SHARE IT.

Consider Bill Gates.

Rich? Certainly. One of the richest men in the world today.

Powerful? Undoubtedly. The founder and CEO of one of the world's most successful companies. (There's only one brand in the world with better name recognition than Microsoft, and that's Coca-Cola.)

One of the secrets of Microsoft's continued success is that Gates hires extremely bright and creative men and women and then urges them to use their brains and talents to the best of their abilities. This sharing of power has not diminished his company, but instead has built one of the most powerful business organizations on the planet.

As leadership guru John Maxwell has written: "You're meant to be a river; not a reservoir. If you use your power to empower others, your leadership will extend far beyond your grasp."

Maxwell also says that too many leaders make the mistake of thinking they can use their position to force others into seeing their point of view or doing things their way. He writes that "leadership is not a power trip, but about giving power to the people under you. It's about giving them the tools they need to do the job."

2. AWESOME POWER BRINGS WITH IT AWESOME RESPONSIBILITIES.

Some people want power without the responsibility that comes with it. But the reality is that you can't have one without the other. Power, unless it is used to make difficult decisions, is not power at all.

As a professional sports executive, I've been given the power to do whatever is necessary to turn various NBA teams into consistent winners. I've had to trade away some popular players because they didn't fit the team's needs. I've been booed by the fans for some trades I've made, and I've been cheered for others. Other times, I've been forced into making trades because I knew we had no possibility of re-signing a player who wanted to move on. (That's why Shaquille O'Neal is playing in Los Angeles these days.) I've learned that if you want responsibility, you had better be prepared to make tough decisions and take the consequences that often go along with them.

A couple of years ago, an American submarine rammed into a Japanese fishing boat. Several young men were knocked off that fishing boat and drowned. Who took the responsibility for that tragedy? The captain, of course. Was he at the controls? No. But he was the person in command, and he had to accept the fact that he was accountable.

When I think of the responsibility that goes with power, one of the first people who comes to mind is Harry S. Truman. Truman became president when Franklin D. Roosevelt died in 1945, and at the time, the United States was still at war with Japan. Soon after taking office, Truman faced the dilemma of whether or not to use a brand-new and horribly destructive weapon called the atomic bomb. He knew the bomb would kill many thousands of Japanese citizens. But he also knew it could shorten the war and thus save thousands of lives. It was an agonizing decision, but Truman made it. Bombs were dropped on Hiroshima and Nagasaki, and the war ended in a matter of days.

In just about anything you choose to do in life, you'll be given some power, and you will need to use it wisely. For example:

- Parents have to exercise power to discipline their children properly and help them grow into the adults they are capable of being.
- Teachers have to exercise power over their students, or the classroom will degenerate into chaos and learning will be impossible.
- Homemakers have to exercise power over the household budget, cleaning, meals, and everything else that goes into keeping a family running as it should.

I could name several other occupations, but almost every occupation and position I can think of requires some power be attached to it. Without some degree of power, you can't do much of anything at all.

3. POWER CANNOT BE GIVEN AWAY—YOU HAVE TO EARN IT.

How many times has it happened? More than a few, that's for sure. A man (or woman) builds a business from the ground up, turning a loan of a few hundred dollars into a multimillion-dollar corporation. Then, when the time comes for that person to retire, he hands things over to his children.

Unfortunately, the children don't have the same ability— or power—their father had, and they run the business into the ground. The children were put into a position of power before they were ready to handle it. They hadn't earned their shot at running a business, and the results were disastrous.

In the Bible, a perfect example of this is found in the twelfth chapter of 1 Kings. This is the sad story of Rehoboam, the son of Solomon. When Solomon died, Rehoboam became king of Israel. But because he was young and lacked experience, he didn't know how to govern. Unfortunately, he listened to advisors who told him to tell his subjects, "My father laid on you a heavy yoke; I will make it even heavier. My father scourged you with whips; I will scourge you with scorpions" (1 Kings 12:11). Rehoboam's intention was to let everyone know that he was in power and that he wasn't going to be pushed around. But it didn't work.

Instead it touched off a rebellion. The people of Israel chose another man, Jeroboam, to be their king, and only Rehoboam's home tribe of Judah remained loyal to him. The result was a permanently divided kingdom. This never would have happened if Rehoboam had the experience needed to handle the power he received when his father died.

One of the most important influences in my life was R. E. Littlejohn, a man who owned the first sports franchise I ever worked for—the minor league Spartanburg Phillies in South Carolina. One of the things he told me, over and over again, was "You've got to pay your dues." How true! If you're going to climb the ladder to the top of your profession, you must do it one rung at a time. That's the only way you can be sure you belong at the top— and that you'll stay there.

> The measure of a man is what he does with power.
>
> PITTACUS, PHILOSOPHER

As I've talked to young people throughout the country, I've found that many of them want to be put in powerful positions as soon as they get out of school. They are impatient. They want power and they want it now. But as the story of Rehoboam shows, assuming a position of power before you're ready can bring about disaster for everyone involved.

I understand the tendency to be impatient. After all, we live in an increasingly fast society. Microwaves cook our food in a small fraction of the time it used to take. E-mail allows us to send text, photos, and other material almost anywhere in the world in an instant. We have instant potatoes, instant coffee, and instant pudding.

But even in this "instant age" there's no such thing as instant power. If you want to be truly powerful, you've got to take the time to earn it. You might even have to stay in the background a little longer than you'd like. But if you are persistent and constantly strive to do a good job, your day will come.

If you're a football fan, I'm sure you know the names of people like Kurt Warner, Brett Favre, Jerry Rice, Tony Gonzales, and Ricky Watters. But have you ever heard of Mack Strong? Strong is a fullback with the Seattle Seahawks. It's his blocking that helps Watters run wild.

> Power flows to the man who knows how. Responsibilities gravitate to the person who can shoulder them.
>
> ELBERT HUBBARD, AUTHOR

An appreciative Watters says, "Mack does all the dirty work in the run game. He does everything. I mean, if the goal posts fell, I wouldn't be surprised to see him go over there and hold them up."

As a result of his "behind the scenes" efforts, Strong recently was named to *USA Today*'s "All-Joes Team." This honor is given annually to men who are willing to sacrifice their own egos for the good of their teams.

You don't have to go around telling everyone how important or powerful you are. If you're powerful, it will get noticed. I really like what former British Prime Minister Margaret Thatcher said: "Being in power is like being a lady. If you have to tell people you are, you aren't."

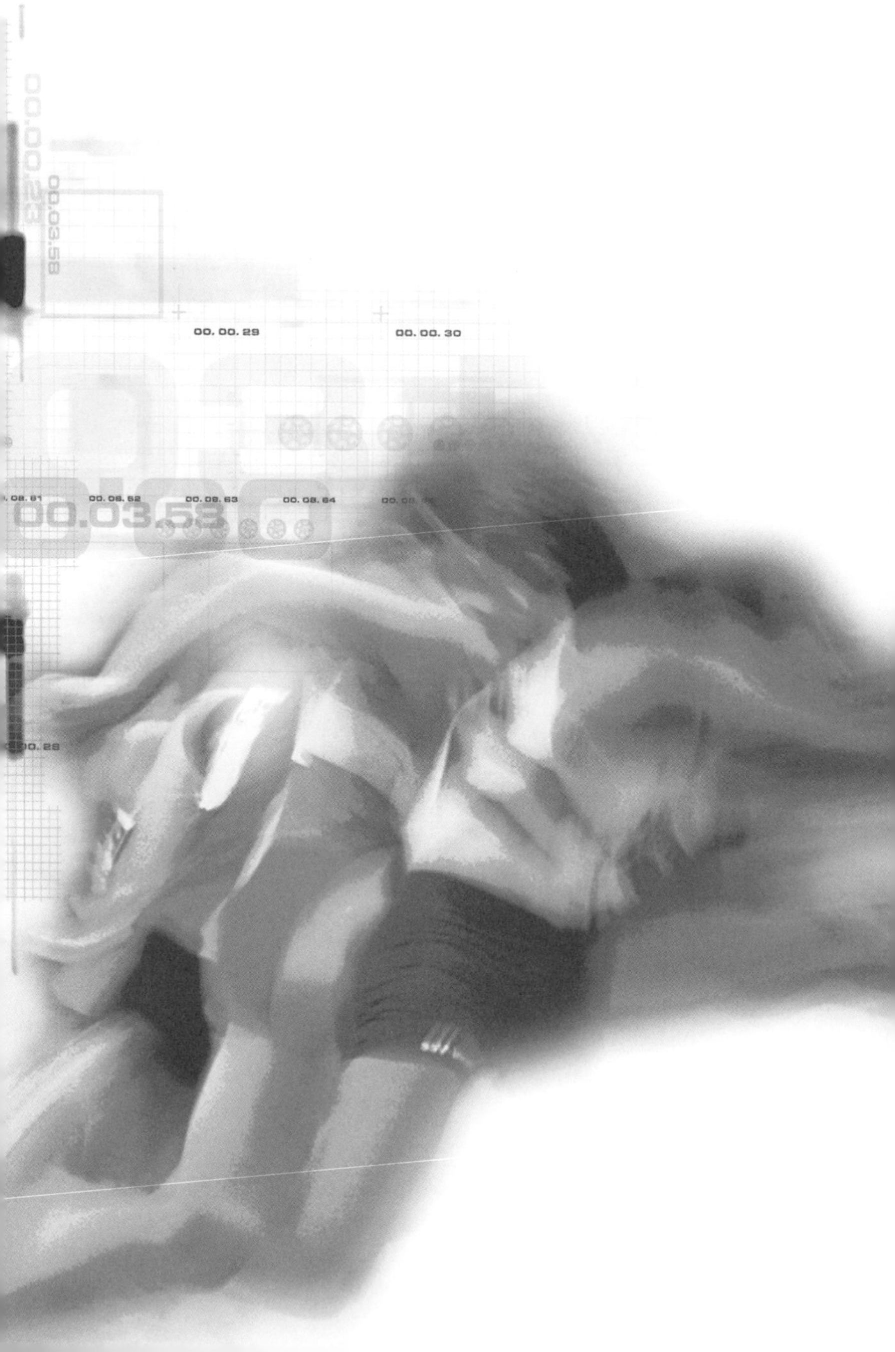
00.00.29
00.00.30
00.03.58

4. In order for power to be of any benefit, you have to use it.

Let me take a moment to tell you about a powerful woman. Her name is Mary Thomas, and in the 1960s she was a single mom trying to raise nine children in a gang-infested area on the west side of Chicago.

The youngest of those children was a five-year-old boy named Isiah.

Late one summer night in 1966, the doorbell rang. When Mary opened the door, she found herself face to face with the leader of the one of the most dangerous gangs in the area, the Vice Lords. Behind him stood the rest of the gang, all wearing black capes and gold tams. Some of the young men had guns in their waistbands.

"We want your boys," the gang leader said. "They can't walk around here and not be in a gang."

Mary shook her head. "There's only one gang around here," she said. "That's the Thomas gang, and I lead that."

She shut the door, but the Vice Lords made no move to leave. She strode through the living room, where the rest of the family sat. Isiah trembled with fear as his mother went into a bedroom and came back out carrying a sawed-off shotgun.

She went to the door, opened it, and pointed the gun at the midsection of the Vice Lords chieftain. "Get off my porch or I'll blow you 'cross the expressway," she shouted. The leader stood there for a moment, but he could tell by the look on her face that she meant what she had said. He turned away, and he and his gang disappeared into the night.

Isiah has never forgotten his mother's confrontation with the Vice Lords. Her example kept him away from drugs, gangs, violence, and other things that could've ruined his life. Today, retired from a successful career as a player in the NBA, Isiah Thomas is head coach of the Indiana Pacers. But who knows where he would be if not for his mother's power—and her powerful example.

Power will be of absolutely no benefit if you don't use it. But when I say that, I'm not suggesting you should try to throw your weight around or "pull rank" on people to get them to do what you want them to do. What I'm saying is that if you're given power in a certain situation, God expects you to use it—for the good of all concerned.

> Power is the capacity to translate intention into reality and sustain it.
>
> WARREN BENNIS,
> LEADERSHIP EXPERT

College president Dr. John C. Bowling says that "a proper view of others keeps one's view of power in line." In other words, if you understand that other people are important, and if you strive to follow Christ's command to love your neighbor as you love yourself, you will be sure to use power wisely, as God intends.

5. THERE IS ONLY ONE SOURCE OF REAL POWER.

When Frances Havergal was a young woman, she had a terrible temper. It didn't take much for her to explode into

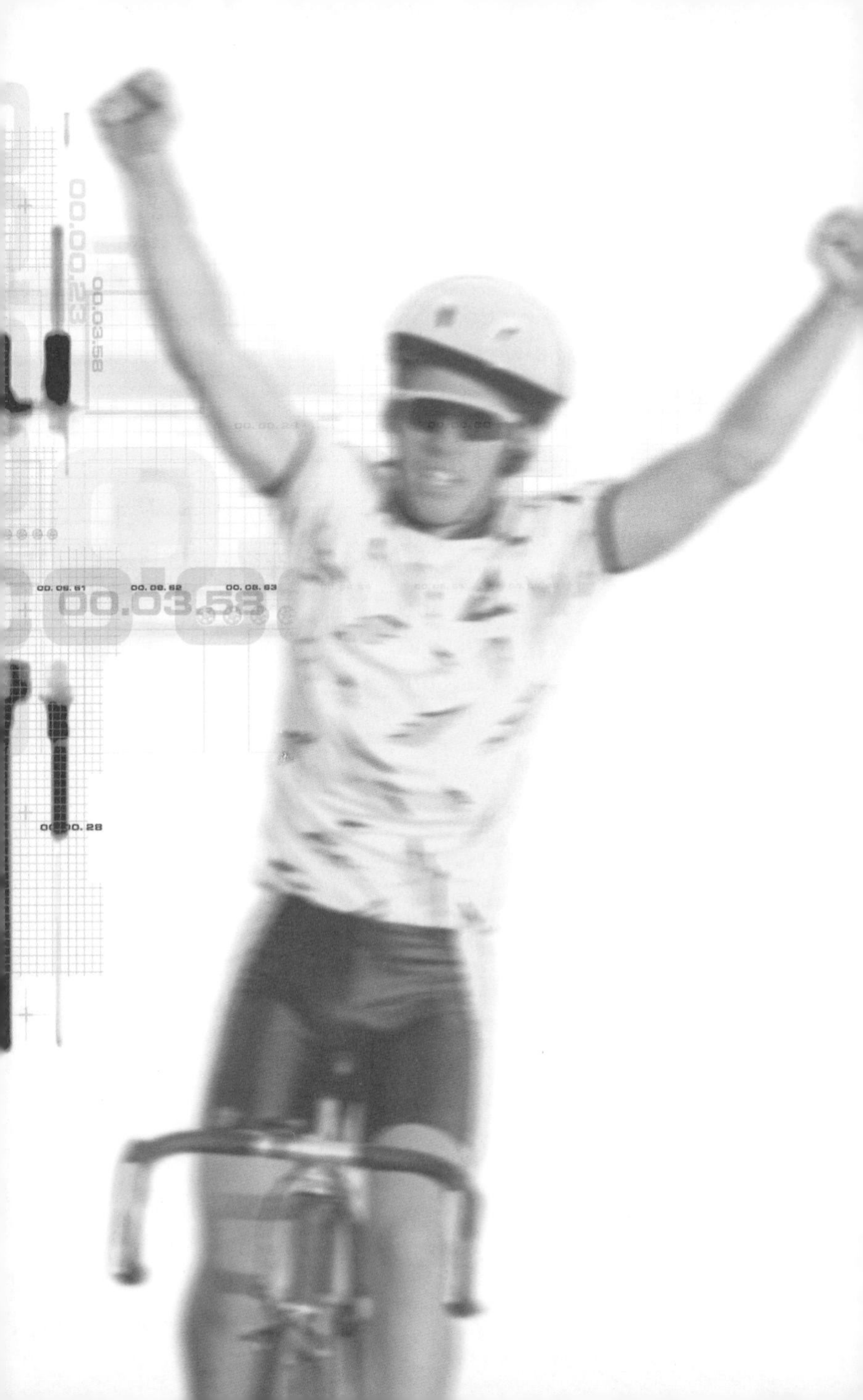
00.00.23
00.03.58
00. 08. 61
00. 08. 62
00. 08. 63
00.03.58

a violent rage. Afterward, she'd always be embarrassed and ashamed of the way she'd acted, and she'd pray that the Lord would help her learn to control herself.

But the next time something happened, there she'd go again!

What made things even worse for Frances was that she was a devout Christian with a growing reputation for writing beautiful worship songs.

One day after a particularly nasty fit of temper, the young songwriter threw herself down on her bed and wept. "Lord," she cried, "will I always be this way?"

As if in immediate reply, a verse from the Bible ran through her mind: "The Egyptians whom ye have seen to day, ye shall see them again no more for ever" (Exod. 14:13 KJV). God had spoken these words to Moses as he led the Israelites out of slavery in Egypt and toward the Promised Land. And Frances felt certain those words contained a message for her. "Lord, forever?" she asked.

> If we have put our faith in Christ, we, too, are connected to a power source . . . the Holy Spirit, Who works in us to make us more like Jesus.
>
> OUR DAILY BREAD

In her mind, she heard the still, small voice of God.

"Yes. No more, forever."

Those who knew her best, including her sister, said that from that day on, Frances never again lost her temper. She had come face to face with the power of God, and her life was never the same! She went on to write many famous hymns, including *Take My Life and Let It Be* and *Like a River Glorious*.

The main thing I want you to take away from this story is that the same power that calmed Frances Havergal's horrible temper is available to you and me today. After all, Jesus himself said, "Apart from me you can do nothing" and "If a man remains in me and I in him, he will bear much fruit" (John 15:5). And before Jesus ascended into heaven, he told his disciples to remain in Jerusalem until they had been "clothed with power from on high" (Luke 24:49).

This was fulfilled on the Day of Pentecost, when the Holy Spirit blew into Jerusalem "like a mighty wind," and the apostles began boldly preaching salvation through faith in Christ. (The entire amazing story can be found in the second chapter of Acts.)

Today, the only way to be "clothed with power from on high" is to accept Jesus Christ as your personal Lord and Savior. Just think! You can have the Power that created the universe in your daily life. And that's a power that makes all the military might of the United States look like a couple of firecrackers.

If you've already given your life to Christ, that's wonderful! Congratulations! Cling to him, and he will never let you down.

If you haven't surrendered to Christ, I urge you to do it right now. It's something you can do anywhere, at any time. Simply tell him in your own words that you're sorry for the sins you have committed and that you want him to take control of your life. If you ask sincerely, he will respond.

And your life will never be the same.

FIVE

PLEASURE

ARE WE HAVING FUN YET?

*Do not bite at the bait of
pleasure until you know there
is no hook beneath it.*

THOMAS JEFFERSON

THE FOURTH DETOUR that keeps people from achieving true success is the pursuit of pleasure. The writer of the Book of Ecclesiastes tried this approach to life, but found it led to disappointment. He wrote:

> I denied myself nothing my eyes desired;
>   I refused my heart no pleasure.
> My heart took delight in all my work,
>   and this was the reward for all my labor.
> Yet when I surveyed all that my hands had done
>   and what I had toiled to achieve,
> everything was meaningless, a chasing after the wind;
>   nothing was gained under the sun.
>
> ECCLESIASTES 2:10–11

Several years ago, a new restaurant in south Florida sent out this "invitation" to nearby residents. I've saved it all this time because I think whoever wrote it did a near-perfect job of appealing to people's desire for pleasure. It reads:

> By the time you finish reading this letter your heart will be pounding, your pulse will be racing, your imagination will be soaring, and your hand will be writing a check for membership in a new private club destined to bring you happiness, success and, possibly, a lifetime of eternal youth. Our bartenders will pour drinks with light hearts and heavy

hands. We'll have music. And dancing. We'll have dashing young attorneys falling madly in love with smashing young stewardesses. We'll have husbands actually holding hands with wives. We'll have quiet moments by crackling fireplaces. And brilliant conversation at the bars. We'll have plenty of parking. And lunch. And dinner. And cocktail hour. And late-night breakfast. We'll have parties when the Dolphins win. We'll have parties when the Dolphins lose. And if that's not enough, we hope to have something that every club in this town should give its right arm for. YOU! The first drink is on us.

Wow! Does that sound like a good time or what? Would it make you happy to spend a carefree evening in a place like that? Maybe. For about fifteen minutes. But then it would all be over, and you'd have to go looking for pleasure somewhere else.

Don't get me wrong. Pleasure is a gift from God, and, as such, there is a place for it in our lives. But if it becomes the be-all and end-all of our existence, pleasure will eventually destroy us.

Some people spend their whole lives chasing after pleasure, and in the process overlook the little delights that God places in their paths every single day. These people are so busy wanting *things* that they never take time to appreciate what they have.

I recently heard about a college professor who asked his students to make a list of what they thought were the current Seven Wonders of the World. The winners were:

- Egypt's pyramids
- The Taj Mahal

- The Grand Canyon
- The Panama Canal
- The Empire State Building
- St. Peter's Basilica
- China's Great Wall

While he was gathering the votes, the professor noted that one student hadn't finished writing. She seemed to be deep in thought, so he asked her if she was having trouble.

"Yes," she replied, "a little. I can't quite make up my mind because there are so many."

The professor said, "Well, why don't you read to us what you have so far, and maybe we can help."

The girl nodded, cleared her throat, and began reading her list of the world's Seven Wonders.

- the ability to touch
- the ability to taste
- the ability to see
- the ability to hear
- the ability to feel
- the ability to laugh
- the ability to love

The classroom grew quiet as everyone thought about the truth they'd just heard. This young lady understood the importance of appreciating what she had—of finding pleasure in the "ordinary" things of life.

Here are some other important truths about the pursuit of pleasure:

1. DON'T MISTAKE PLEASURE FOR JOY.

Writer Henry Bosch explains the difference between pleasure and joy: "Pleasure is dependent on circumstances, but joy is inward and is not disturbed by one's environment. Pleasure is always changing, but joy is constant. Pleasure is built on self-seeking, but joy is based on self-sacrifice."

He goes on to say, "To keep experiencing pleasure, we must run from one stimulus to another, for it refuses to be permanently grasped. Joy is just the opposite. It is a gift we receive from God."

True joy comes from a relationship with God, who is constant—the same yesterday, today, and forever. Joy is an inner peace and contentment. It's closely related to happiness, although it isn't the same thing. You can be joyful even on a day when you're not particularly happy—such as on a morning when it's pouring rain and you've had a flat tire on your way to work.

And although joy is a gift from God, it's also the result of a positive attitude. In other words, if you make up your mind to be joyful, I believe God will increase your joy and bring you to the point where a joyful attitude is just part of your natural state of being. That's why the apostle Paul wrote: "Rejoice in the Lord always. I will say it again: Rejoice!" (Phil. 4:4). And: "Whatever is true, whatever is noble, whatever is right, whatever is pure, whatever is lovely, whatever is admirable—if anything is excellent or praiseworthy—think about such things" (Phil. 4:8).

Those verses remind me of a story about a woman named Maurine Jones.

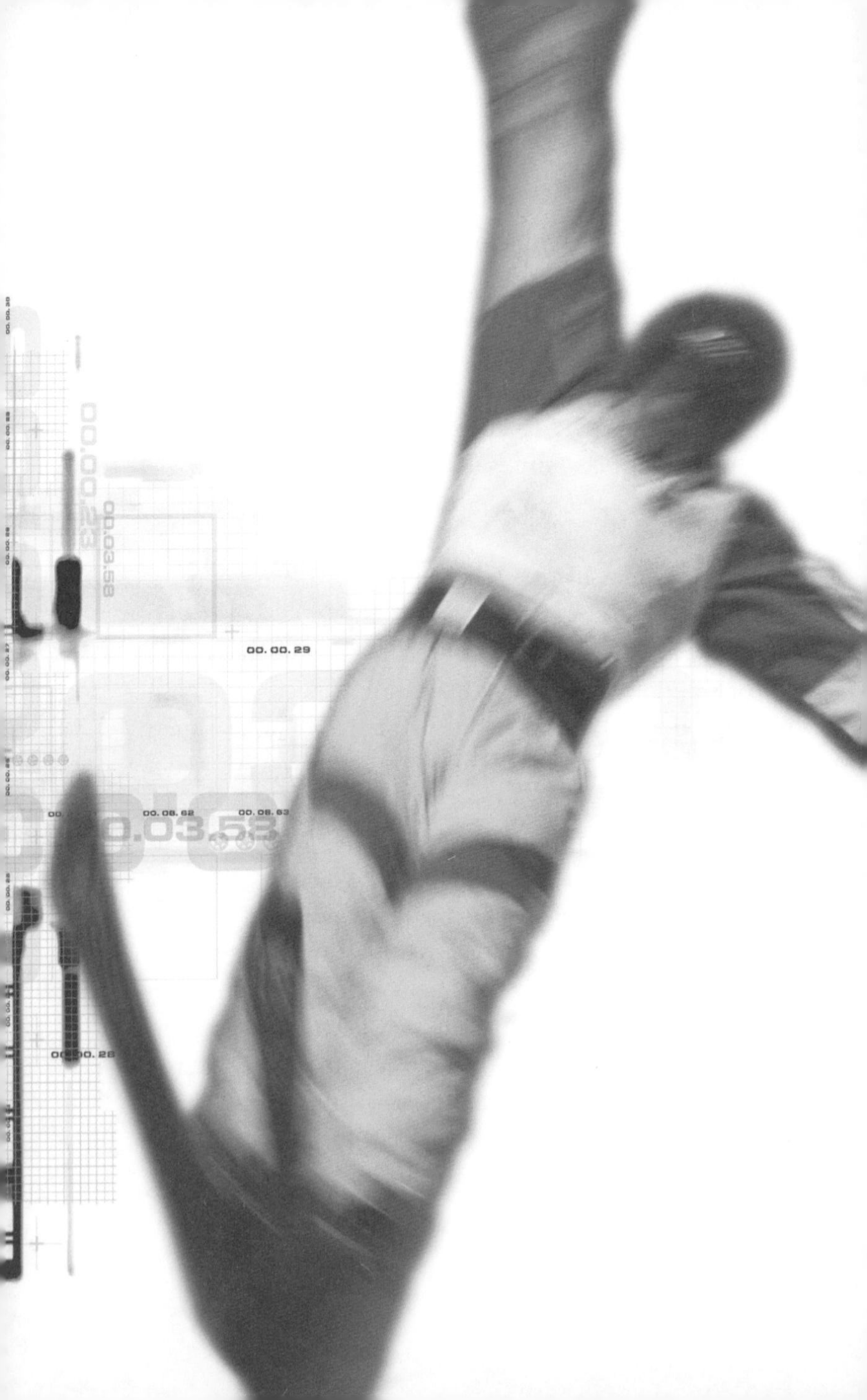
00. 00. 29
00. 08. 62
00. 08. 63

Mrs. Jones is ninety-two. Her husband of seventy years recently passed away, making it necessary for her to move to a nursing home.

A friend describes Mrs. Jones as a lovely, gracious, dignified woman. "She is fully dressed each morning by eight o'clock, with her hair fashionably coiffed and makeup perfectly applied, even though she is legally blind."

Her friend was there to help Mrs. Jones move into the nursing home. After many hours of waiting patiently, Mrs. Jones smiled sweetly when told her room was ready. As she maneuvered her walker to the elevator, her friend provided a visual description of the tiny room, including the eyelet sheets that had been hung on the window.

> I've never been a good parent or a good husband. Now I'm a guilty old man who's ashamed of the kind of life I've led.
>
> MARLON BRANDO

"I love it," Mrs. Jones stated with the enthusiasm of an eight-year-old just presented with a new puppy.

"But Mrs. Jones," the friend said, "you haven't seen the room . . . just wait."

"That doesn't have anything to do with it," Mrs. Jones replied. "Whether I like my room or not doesn't depend on how the furniture is arranged. It's how I arrange my mind. I already decided to love it."

She continued, "It's a decision I make every morning when I wake up. I have a choice; I can spend the day in bed recounting the difficulty I have with the parts of my body that no longer work, or I can get out of bed and be thankful for the ones that do. Each day is a gift, and as long as my eyes open, I'll focus on the new day and all the happy memories I've stored away."

Is it a pleasure to be ninety-two years old? I'll let you know when I get there . . . but I doubt it. At sixty-two, I already take a lot longer to get in shape for a marathon than I used to.

Is it a pleasure losing your mate? Of course not. How about living in a nursing home? Not exactly something you look forward to, is it?

And yet Maurine Jones made up her mind that she was going to find pleasure in whatever life brought her. And you know something? A joyous attitude is contagious. When you work at developing an attitude like the one demonstrated by Mrs. Jones, people are going to like being around you—and that's going to have a positive impact on how successful you are in life.

2. Pleasure can lead to pain.

How sad to be an old man looking back on his life and seeing that it was filled with self-indulgence and missteps. What a contrast to the attitude expressed by Maurine Jones!

Marlon Brando was one of the great actors of his day— an Academy Award winner admired and respected as one of the best in his field. He made more money for a few weeks' work than most of us will ever see in our lifetimes. But now, instead of looking back with pride on all he was able to accomplish, he says that he is "ashamed" of the life he's lived.

I'm not saying that Marlon Brando's assessment of his life is accurate. Only he and God know that. But it is true that a life spent in the pursuit of pleasure often ends up in sorrow and pain.

History is full of examples.

Elvis Presley, "The King of Rock 'n' Roll," died at age forty-two, a bloated caricature of a man who'd ruined his life with drugs and reckless living.

Bill Clinton very nearly destroyed his presidency because of his pursuit of sexual pleasure, and certainly tarnished the way history will regard him.

John Belushi destroyed his life seeking pleasure through drugs.

So did **Chris Farley**.

And **Jimi Hendrix**.

And on and on the list goes.

When I was a child, I sometimes wondered why my mother wouldn't let me eat all the candy I wanted. I thought, "When I grow up, I'm not going to eat anything but candy. Except maybe for an ice-cream cone once in a while."

Can you imagine what I'd look like if I never ate anything but ice cream and candy? I'd weigh about five hundred pounds, for one thing. And most of my teeth would've rotted out by now. I had to learn to eat a lot of things I didn't particularly like, because they were good for me. And now—guess what? I've discovered that I actually like a lot of those things!

That's the way it is in life. It's not good to spend all your time having fun. Rest all the time and your muscles will atrophy. Spend all your time reading comic books and watching sitcoms and your intellect will weaken. Spend too much time eating and you'll be dangerously over-weight. Drink too much and you'll become an alcoholic.

Be careful not to let the goodness of life elude you. Begin to build the sort of life you will look back on with pride when you're ninety years old!

3. SOME PEOPLE AMUSE THEMSELVES TO DEATH.

Just about every big city in the United States has a rescue mission. A mission is a Christian ministry that reaches out to bring God's love to homeless people. Missions get people off the streets, introduce them to the possibility of new life through faith in Jesus Christ, and then strive to help them become productive, contributing members of society.

I have nothing but admiration for anyone who works in a rescue mission. These people definitely have to be called by God, because running one can be a very difficult, dangerous, and frustrating job. If you run a rescue mission, you need a very forgiving spirit.

There are many reasons why people wind up homeless. But if you talk to the folks who've been rescued from the streets by a mission and ask them how they became homeless, a large majority will tell you it's because they're addicted to drugs or alcohol. For most of them, the downward spiral to the streets began with cocaine—either powder or crack.

They didn't start taking drugs because they knew they'd wind up homeless. They took drugs because they wanted to have fun. They were merely amusing themselves! But when drugs took control, they gave up everything in an attempt to satisfy their habit. They cut themselves off from friends and family because nothing mattered but the next high. Some of them stole from their parents to buy drugs. Others resorted to burglary, armed robbery, and, of course, drug dealing. They "amused" themselves into poverty, loneliness, and despair. And without help, they will continue to seek the pleasure of drugs until it kills them.

I can think of another place where the pursuit of pleasure is proving deadly: sub-Saharan Africa.

In that part of the world, there are more than 13.2 million orphans living all by themselves. Almost all of them have lost their parents to AIDS. According to the United Nations, there may be as many as 40 million orphans by the end of 2010.

> What our deepest self craves is not mere enjoyment, but some supreme purpose that will enlist all our powers and will give unity and direction to our life. We can never know the profoundest joy without a conviction that our life is significant . . . not a meaningless episode.
>
> HENRY J. GOLDING, AUTHOR

What's caused this deadly epidemic? Sexual promiscuity. Those who promote "free love" used to ask, "What harm can come from sex between two consenting adults?" Now we know.

So we see that some people are killing themselves by pursuing pleasure through drugs, while others are dying by

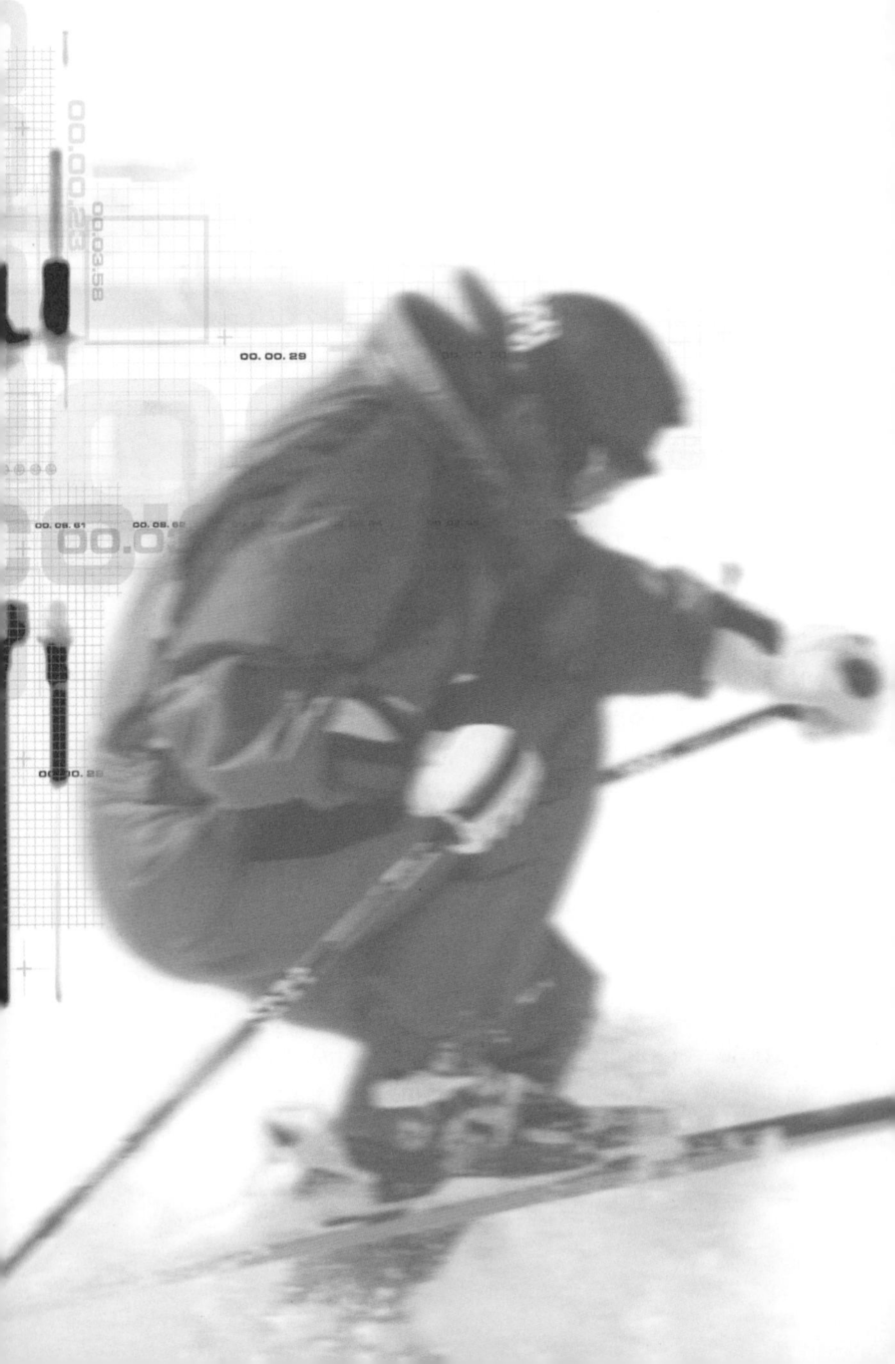

pursuing pleasure through illicit sex. But there are also those who are killing themselves slowly by spending their lives finding ways to have fun. By never taking the time to be quiet and listen for God's voice. By never trying to figure out what life is all about.

I recently came across an article about my good friend Mike Schmidt, the Hall of Fame slugger who played third base for the Philadelphia Phillies during much of the seventies and eighties. In addition to being a superb athlete, Schmidt is an all-around good guy—a solid Christian who came to know the Lord when I was coordinating the Phillies's chapel services. I admired him so much that I named one of my sons after him.

Even though he's financially set for the rest of his life, Schmidt recently rejoined the Phillies temporarily as a spring training hitting instructor. In the article I read, Schmidt talked about how happy he is to be back with the Phillies. He told *USA Today* columnist Hal Bodley, "I've had some great, wonderful times traveling, playing golf, fishing, and just being totally retired," but then added that a "lack of purpose" sometimes left him feeling bored and stressed out. "I don't feel a lot of substance in my life," he said. "It's like I'm living my life just for me."

You see, living only for yourself—or only for pleasure—can leave you feeling discontented and unsatisfied.

> Many people have had to learn in their private lives, and nations have had to learn in their historical experience, that perhaps the worst form of tragedy is wanting something badly, getting it, and finding it empty.
>
> HENRY KISSINGER

4. Sometimes you can find pleasure in the least-expected places.

Years ago, we had a live-in nanny named Mary. (With nineteen children, we *had* to have a live-in nanny!) Every night at eleven o'clock, after the kids were in bed, Mary would come out dressed to the nines, ready to start her evening.

I'd always ask her, "Where you headed tonight?"

And every night, her answer was the same. She was going out to a nightclub in hopes of meeting "somebody interesting."

"Well, have you ever met anyone interesting in a place like that?" I'd ask.

"No."

"Then why do you keep going there?"

Mary would just smile that mischievous smile of hers and say, "Well, you never know."

I'd sometimes playfully urge her to seek pleasure in other things. "Why don't you stay home tonight and read a good book?" I'd ask. Or "Why don't you stay in and get a good night's sleep?"

But she wouldn't hear of it. She was running full-speed ahead after an elusive something. But sadly, as far as I know, she never found it.

How many people do you know who are living their lives this way?

In contrast, Mother Teresa spent most of her life working among the poor and sick in the slums of Calcutta.

Someone once said to her, "I wouldn't do what you do for a million dollars."

Her reply? "Neither would I!"

She didn't see her work as something painful and awful. Yes, it was heartbreaking. Yes, it was difficult beyond what most of us could ever imagine. But even so, Mother Teresa found pleasure in knowing that she was taking God's love and mercy to people living in sorrow, poverty, and pain.

It's true. Pleasure can be found in the most unexpected places. Years ago, there was a television show called *Candid Camera.* The theme song contained these words: "When it's least expected, you're elected, you're the star today. Smile, you're on *Candid Camera.*"

That's the way it is with pleasure. If you're seeking God and trying to follow his will for your life, you may be surprised to discover that you're having fun. I believe God wants us all to have fun, but he expects us to find that fun in wholesome, healthy ways. That's the sort of "pleasure" I'm surrounded by, living right in the middle of one of America's premier vacation destinations. Florida's beaches aren't far away, and I'm only a few minutes from Disney World, SeaWorld, Universal Studios, and several other top-notch attractions. People come here on vacation because they need a break from the pressures of daily life. God understands that. He's not a spoilsport who wants to see you miserable. He just wants you to have your fun in ways that are good for you.

So far, we've discussed four detours that keep people from achieving true success in life. Those detours are:

1. The pursuit of money
2. The pursuit of fame
3. The pursuit of power
4. The pursuit of pleasure

I'd like to wrap up this book by discussing how you can find true success in life. But first, I want to spend a few pages on something that's rather unpleasant, but also very important. It's something we'll all face at one point, and thus, something we all need to be ready for.

It's called . . . death.

SIX

00. 00. 29   00. 00. 30

IMMORTALITY

ONE WAY TO FOREVER

What worries me is that when I get to the pearly gates and they look at the things I've done in my life, what are they going to say? That's my number one worry.

JERRY LEE LEWIS, SINGER

MOST YOUNG ADULTS don't spend much time thinking about death. After all, death seems to be a long, long way away. They know it's going to come eventually, but it hardly seems real when they're strong, healthy, and full of life.

That's why many young people drive fast and live recklessly. They feel immortal.

Perhaps this has changed somewhat since the terrorist attack on the World Trade Center. I hope so. Not because I think anyone should live in constant fear of death. But since death is one of life's most important events, it is never too early to begin preparing for it. In fact, I believe that if you are prepared for it, death is not something to be feared at all. Rather, it is something to be welcomed as a transitional period to another, better state of being.

As psychiatrist Charles L. Allen wrote:

We need not fear death, because God is the God He is. Think of how wise and tender God is. When He brought us into this world, He planned it so beautifully. Can you think of a better way to be born, than into the bosom of a Mother? God made Mothers and, if God so planned our birth in such a lovely fashion, we can be assured He has planned our entrance into eternity in a tender and glorious manner.

Before we reach the end of this chapter, I will discuss some important steps you can take to overcome the fear of death. But first, there are four important truths about death I want you to know:

1. THE WAY YOU LIVE DETERMINES HOW YOU DIE.

There's a Middle Eastern blessing that says, "When you were born, you cried and the world rejoiced. May you live your life so that when you die, the world will cry and you will rejoice."

Someone else has put it this way: "To live a worthwhile life, you should know, early on, what you want written on your tombstone."

I also really like what Martin Luther King Jr. said: "The minute you conquer the fear of death . . . at that moment, you are free. I submit to you that if a man hasn't discovered something that he will die for, he isn't fit to live."

King was frightened when he first felt called to be involved in the Civil Rights movement. He was a young man, newly married and fresh out of seminary. He knew he would be putting his life on the line if he stood up for the rights of black Americans, and this made him afraid.

But as he wrestled with God in prayer one night, a peace descended upon him. The fear of death left him and never returned. It wasn't as if he felt protected from those who wanted to take his life. But rather he felt that God would be with him no matter what happened.

A fearless King even told his supporters:

Every now and then I think about my own death, and I think about my own funeral. . . . and I don't want a long funeral. If you get somebody to deliver the eulogy, tell them not to talk too long. . . . Say that I was a drum major for justice. Say that I was a drum major for peace, that I was a drum major for righteousness, and all of the other shallow things will not matter. I won't have any money to leave behind. I won't have the fine and luxurious things of life to leave behind, but I just want to leave a committed life behind.

Someone once said, "When it comes time to die, make sure all you've got to do is die." In other words:

- Do your best to live at peace with everyone, so that you are not tormented on your deathbed with the knowledge that you have things to set right.
- If you need to forgive someone, do it now, before it's too late.
- If you need to ask someone's forgiveness, again, do it now.
- If there's something you need to say to someone, don't put it off.
- Whatever you need to do, do it now instead of waiting for "someday." "Someday" rarely comes.

In David Ringer's book *Looking Out for Number One,* the author tells the story of a New York stockbroker who had built a fortune worth more than fifty million. Then the man discovered he had a terminal disease and had only a few months to live. "Life has played a trick on me," he said bitterly. "All my plans and preparations were for living—I am not prepared for death."

How about you? Are you living a life that prepares you for death?

2. DEATH CAN COME AT ANY TIME, SO BE PREPARED.

In 1997, I spoke at a convention in Detroit shortly after the Red Wings had won the Stanley Cup. Everywhere I went, people were wearing Red Wings's shirts and caps. Flags and banners flew everywhere in the city.

On my way back to the airport after my speech, the driver was talking about—what else?—the Red Wings and how good they were. He especially raved about the five Russians on the team.

The next morning when I was back home in Orlando, I was stunned to see that one of those Russian players had been seriously injured in an automobile accident. The car in which he had been a passenger had gone off the highway and hit a tree. The player, Vladimir Konstantinov, had suffered severe injuries and was fighting for his life.

> Everybody has got to die, but I have always believed an exception would be made in my case. Now what?
>
> WILLIAM SAROYAN, AUTHOR, DAYS BEFORE HE DIED OF CANCER

Once again, I was reminded of how fragile life is. None of us knows what the next moment will bring.

Author W. Somerset Maugham once said, "Death is a dull, dreary affair, and my advice to you is to have nothing whatever to do with it."

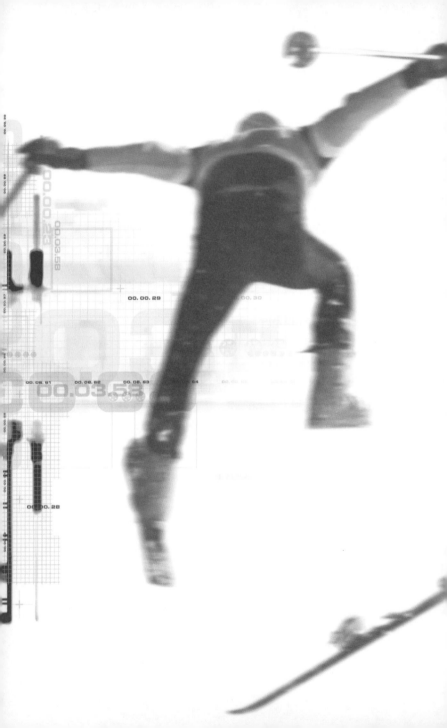

Woody Allen echoed this when he said, "I don't want to achieve immortality through my work. I want to achieve immortality by not dying."

These quotes make us smile, of course. But the fact is, no matter how much we may want to avoid death, we simply can't do it. The Bible says, "It is appointed unto a man once to die, but after this the judgment" (Heb. 9:27 KJV). We're all going to die, and the sooner we make peace with that fact, the happier we will be.

Think of how often we face death every day.

- If you go outside in a rainstorm, you might be struck by lightning.
- If you go for a spin in a car, you might get in a terrible accident.
- If you take a trip by airplane, you might crash.
- If you go for a walk, you might get hit by a car.
- If you go for a few laps in the pool, you might drown.

Okay, I admit it. I'm being melodramatic and more than a bit morbid. But my point is that death could come to any of us at any time. None of us has any idea how many times the Lord—or one of his angels—has protected us because it wasn't our time to go.

A few years ago, a church in a small town was ripped apart by a gas leak just a few minutes past seven o'clock on a Tuesday night. The explosion occurred just a few minutes after choir practice was scheduled to begin.

Fire trucks, ambulances, and police cars raced to the scene. The blast had demolished the church, and it was apparent that no one inside the building could've survived. But you know what? Not a single person was injured. That's because every member of the choir was late for practice that evening. Later on, as the members of the choir pieced together their stories, they realized God had intervened in each one of their lives.

One man's car wouldn't start. One woman's baby-sitter was late. Another was walking out the door when her telephone rang. And so it went, with each survivor recounting some specific occurrence that prevented him or her from getting to the church on time!

That's an amazing story. But I believe God does that sort of thing for us all the time. Who knows? Maybe that annoying telemarketing call that made you late for an appointment also kept you from being struck down by a drunk driver.

We'll never know this side of heaven all the times God has rescued us from impending doom. But sooner or later, the time to die is going to come. And that will be quickly followed by the time of judgment.

Former coach of the Washington Redskins Joe Gibbs says, "The evidence is in. Life is a gift. It's fragile, and it can be taken away in a single tick of the clock—and the clock is running. When the final second ticks away for you, you want to be sure that you are on the winning team."

3. Those who are prepared to die are prepared to live.

In December of 1862, 6,300 Union soldiers were killed or wounded in the Battle of Fredericksburg. When night fell and the sounds of battle faded, the air became filled with the moans and cries of wounded and dying men.

The wailing continued through the night until the sun came up the following morning. By that time, a nineteen-year-old Confederate sergeant named Richard R. Kirkland felt he couldn't take it anymore. He went to his commander and said, "Sir, I'd like to take those boys some water."

"Son," came the reply, "you're a fool."

> Let us endeavor so to live that, when we come to die, even the undertaker will be sorry.
>
> MARK TWAIN

Despite that response, Kirkland jumped the wall, carrying a canteen full of cool water to the open field where the wounded lay. He was greeted by a burst of gunfire from the Union side of the field. But then, as Kirkland knelt down and gave a suffering Union soldier a drink of refreshing water, the astonished Union commander ordered his men to hold their fire.

In awe, the Union officer raised his hand and shouted to his troops. "Don't shoot that man! He's too brave to die!"

Have you ever seen such an act of bravery? Have you ever wondered how some people can be fearless, while others seem to live in constant fear—always looking over their shoulders, always afraid of what tomorrow will bring?

A few months before Marilyn Monroe died from a drug overdose, she wrote these words in a notebook: "What am I afraid of? Why am I so afraid? Do I think I can't act? I know I can act, but I am afraid. I am afraid and I should not be and I must not be."

Apparently, the beautiful actress, one of the most admired women in the world, was not able to heed her own positive self-talk. Marilyn was afraid to live, so she gave up.

More recently, a superstar named Madonna said, "The truth scares me. Being alone scares me. Failure scares me. Dying scares me. I don't think I'm different from anyone else."

Certainly, we live in a time of widespread fear, especially in light of the terrorist attacks on the United States and the resultant war in Afghanistan. But even in these uncertain times, those who understand that dying is not an end, but rather a beginning, can live without fear. Only those who know the peace and comfort God's love imparts can be truly ready to live, and thus, truly ready to die.

I am reminded of an amazing story I recently read about a girl named Hawa Ahmed. Hawa was a Muslim girl living in North Africa when she read a Christian tract and decided to give her life to Christ. When her father and brothers found out about this, they decided to do what they felt Allah wanted them to do.

They decided to kill her.

They bound her to a chair fixed to a metal plate, with which they planned to electrocute her. The frightened girl asked her father if he would at least allow her to die with a Bible in her lap. He responded, "If you want to die together with your false religion, so be it." With a sneer, one of her brothers added, "That will show you that your religion is powerless."

Hawa later told her friends that when the Bible was placed on her lap, peace flooded through her. She knew she was going to die. And she was ready.

But she didn't die!

Four times, her father and brothers tried to electrocute her, but nothing happened. Finally her exasperated father untied her, hit her, and screamed, "You are no longer my daughter!" Then he threw her out into the street.

Humiliated and naked, Hawa ran through the crowded streets to the nearby home of a Christian friend, who took her in and clothed her.

The next day, when the friend asked Hawa's neighbors what they had thought when they saw Hawa running naked through the streets, they replied, "Naked? What are you talking about? She was wearing a beautiful white dress." Someone else said, "We were wondering why someone in such a beautiful dress would be running through the streets like that."

Hawa was prepared to die, but God had clothed her in the beauty of his life and love. Today, Hawa has changed her name to Faith and is a full-time evangelist with an organization called Every Home for Christ.

> If you know Christ, before the doctor has a chance to pronounce you dead, you will be in the Lord's presence.
>
> TONY EVANS, AUTHOR

Hawa has lived her life to the fullest. But what does it mean to live life to the fullest? It means to be free to concentrate on the things that are really important, and not be driven by an unhealthy desire for money, fame, power, or pleasure.

Author Sam Shoemaker says that many people make the mistake of spending their lives going to the right schools and trying to make the right grades, so they can get the right jobs, make the right salaries, live in the right neighborhoods, move with the right circles of friends, and vacation in the right places. "And you know where it all ends, don't you? It ends on a little hillside under a tiny plot of sod with a granite tombstone which should read, 'You've pampered yourself into mediocrity when God wanted you to commit yourself to immortality.'"

Someone wise once wrote:

I was dying to finish high school and start college.
Then I was dying to finish college and start working.
Then I was dying to marry and have children.
Then I was dying for my children to grow old enough so
    that I could return to work.
Then I was dying to retire.
Now . . . I am dying,
and suddenly, I realize,
I forgot to live.

You are just starting out in life. Promise yourself right now that you won't forget to live.

4. DEATH CAN BE A REWARD INSTEAD OF A PUNISHMENT.

Max Lucado says that death is often God's way of taking people away from evil. "From what kind of evil? An extended disease? An addiction? A dark season of rebellion? We don't know. But we know that no person lives one day more or less than God intends."

The problem with the "human" view of death is that it's very shortsighted. We see it only from a narrow viewpoint, whereas God sees it from an eternal perspective. You might say that life on earth is only a short test-drive. The real life comes later on—*if* you know Jesus.

I've already provided you with one opportunity to accept Christ as your Lord and Savior. But because accepting Christ is the only way you can be totally prepared to live—and die—I must do it again. Here are some things you need to know:

1. All human beings are separated from God by sin, and there is no way we can reach him on our own.
2. God chose to bridge the gap that separates us by sending his Son to die on our behalf.
3. Everyone has to make a decision. We must say yes or no to Jesus. Those who say yes are cleansed by his blood and made righteous. Those who say no remain separated from God and are without hope. God has done what he can. The rest is up to us.
4. The moment you say yes to Christ, many wonderful things happen to you:
   All your sins are forgiven—past, present, and future (Col. 2:13–14).
   You become a child of God (John 1:12 and Rom. 8:15).
   You receive eternal life (John 5:24).
   Christ comes to dwell within you (Col. 1:27 and Rev. 3:20).
   You become a new creation (2 Cor. 5:17).

You are declared righteous by God (2 Cor. 5:21).
You are accepted by God (Col. 1:19–22).

If you would like to accept Christ right now and know that for you, death will not be a punishment but a reward, you can use this prayer:

Father, I know that I am a sinner. I need Jesus Christ in my life to save me from my sins. Thank you that you love me in spite of the wrong things I have done. I know that it is your grace that saves me, and not anything I can do or say. Jesus, I believe that you suffered and died on my behalf, and that God raised you from the dead. Thank you for being Lord over every area of my life—my thoughts, my actions, and my relationships. Thank you, Father, for saving me! I am a new person in Jesus Christ, and heaven is my home for eternity. I pray all of this in the name of Jesus Christ, my Lord and Savior. Amen.

If you prayed this prayer, please let me know. You can call me at 407-916-2404. I'd like to talk with you as soon as possible about the new life you've just begun.

Believe me, you'll never regret it!

SEVEN

A GAME PLAN
THAT WORKS

Success is the result of perfection, hard work, learning from failure, loyalty and persistence.

COLIN POWELL

WE'VE SPENT A LOT OF TIME discussing what success is not. Now let's talk about what it is. The following "Ten Commandments of Success" have been collected from three important sources:

- wise people who have achieved tremendous success in life
- my own experiences as a father, husband, businessman, and Christian
- God's Word

The first of these Ten Commandments is:

1. SURRENDER CONTROL OF YOUR LIFE TO CHRIST.

"What? He's talking about this again?"

Yes, I am. Because there's nothing more important to talk about. God is the foundation upon which everything else must be built.

Did you attend Vacation Bible School when you were a kid? If so, you probably remember singing the song based on one of the Lord's parables about the foolish man who built his house upon the sand.

Do you remember? "Oh, the rains came down and the floods came up. The rains came down and the floods came up. The rains came down and the floods came up, and the house on the sand went . . . SMASH!"

Well, if you're trying to build a successful life upon anything other than faith in Christ, you *are* building a house on the sand, and it *will* end up crashing all around you.

Jesus told another parable about a man who had it made. He had plenty of land, plenty of cattle, plenty of everything a man could want. And as he looked over his possessions and thought about what to do next, he snapped his fingers and said, "I've got it! I'll tear down these old barns and build bigger ones. Then I can get more stuff because I'll have more room to store it!"

But God had other plans. He knew the man was not going to live to see another sunrise. And he called the man a fool because he knew the man had spent his life focusing on things that had no eternal value. What good would those bigger barns do if he was spending eternity in hell—alone and cut off from God?

Grant Hill, who is one of my favorite basketball players—and not just because he plays for the Orlando Magic—put it this way: "To have everything that this world equates with success and to feel empty inside is pretty amazing. But that's definitely where I once was. If I didn't have Christ in my life, I'd be unhappy. I'd be miserable, although I'd have everything this world says I need to have."

2. SEEK FIRST THE KINGDOM OF GOD.

John D. Rockefeller, who went on to become the richest man in the world, started out as a clerk making $3.75 a week. It wasn't much to live on even then, but he still managed to give half of it to God.

Later on, as Rockefeller was amassing his fortune, he became careless in his giving to God. Then when he was fifty-two years old, he was diagnosed with a serious illness. Doctors told him he had less than a year to live.

While contemplating his own mortality, Rockefeller thought back to the pleasure he had received by giving to his church. He resolved that he would spend his last year giving his money away. He sold half his stock in Standard Oil and began funding worthy causes all over the world. He didn't do it because he was trying to buy God's grace or mercy, but just the same, something strange began to happen. The more he gave away, the better he felt! Soon, his doctor could find no sign of the illness that had threatened his life. He lived to be ninety-one years old and gave away millions and millions of dollars.

By the way, another interesting thing happened. During Rockefeller's last thirty-nine years of life, his remaining Standard Oil stock rose so much in value that he was richer at ninety-one than he had been at fifty-two, when he had started giving his money away.

Dwight L. Moody, one of the greatest evangelists of the nineteenth century, made it a point to pray for at least one hour every morning. The only exception was when the day looked so full that he didn't have time to pray for one hour. Then he prayed for two hours.

He knew that the less time he had, the more time he needed to spend with God. He believed that God would stretch the hours that were left to him—and over the course of his life, he found this to be true.

The same is true of money. Put the kingdom of God first at all times, and God will bless you in more ways than you can imagine.

3. Do unto others as you would have them do unto you.

Can you imagine what a wonderful world this would be if we all measured our actions by the Golden Rule? No lying. No cheating. No stealing. No violence against other people. No businesses cutting hundreds of jobs in order to increase their profits. No employees refusing to give an honest day's work for an honest day's pay.

You might ask: "Pat, isn't it kind of naïve to think we could all live that way?" Maybe. But living in accordance with the Golden Rule has to start somewhere, and it may as well be with you and me. I'm not saying that some people won't try to take advantage of you if they know your motto is "Do unto others as you would have them do unto you." Frankly, being "nice" often puts you in a vulnerable position in a world whose motto is "There's a sucker born every minute." But if you do treat other people well, you'll have two of the most important things any human being can have: peace of mind and treasure in heaven.

Plus, even though baseball manager Leo Durocher said, "Nice guys finish last," I've seen enough to know that this isn't always true. Very often, nice guys finish first. They reach the top of their profession by being honest, ethical, and fair.

After all, successful businessman Charles Schwab said, "Unless you treat your colleagues fairly, you can never be a successful leader."

4. ALWAYS DO YOUR BEST.

In 1934, a young man named John Wooden wrote down his definition of success: "Success is peace of mind, which is a direct result of self-satisfaction in knowing you did your best to become the best that you are capable of becoming."

John Wooden's "effort to do the best" paid off. He became one of the most respected college basketball coaches of all time—and certainly the most successful. But Coach Wooden's success hasn't been confined to the basketball court. He's been a tremendous shaper of young lives as well, instilling good qualities in young men and women that continue to serve them long after their days as college athletes.

When Wooden was twelve years old, his father presented him with a seven-point creed to live by. It's titled "Making the Most of One's Self," and its seven guidelines are as valid today as they were nearly eighty years ago.

1. Be true to yourself.
2. Make each day your masterpiece.
3. Help others.
4. Read good books, especially the Bible.
5. Make friendship a fine art.
6. Build a shelter against a rainy day.

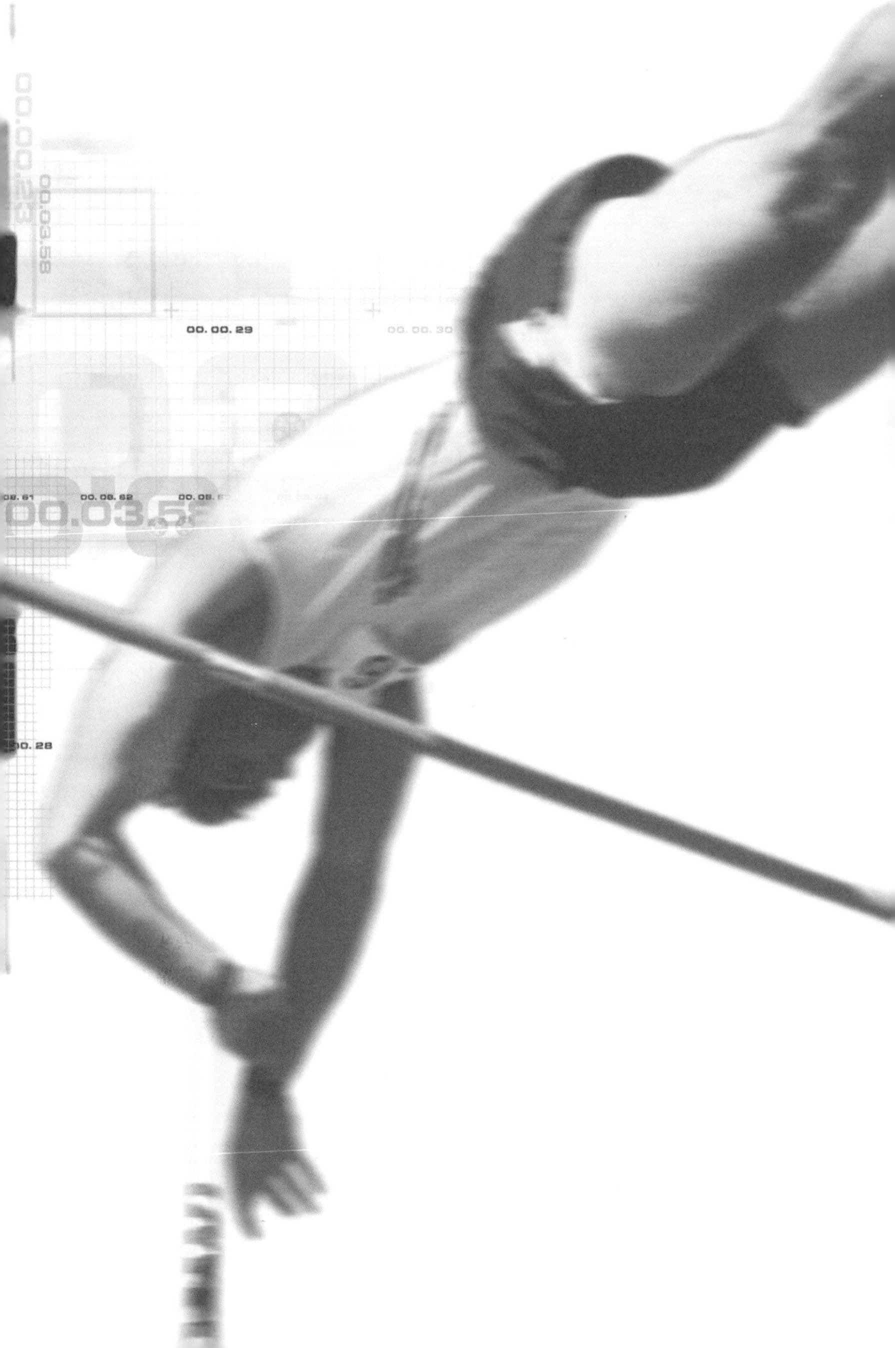

7. Pray for guidance and give thanks for your blessings every day.

If you want to be a success in life, strive to be the best you can be. Grab opportunities when they come your way. And, more than that, make your own opportunities.

Of course, you're not always going to be at your best. There will be times when you aren't hitting on all cylinders because you didn't get enough sleep the night before, or because you had an argument with someone you care about, or because you're just not feeling well. But even during those times, it is possible to say, "I'm doing the best I can, given the circumstances." You don't have to be perfect twenty-four/seven. You just have to do the best you can do. And that's enough.

As singer Amy Grant said: "I have come to see that Christianity is not really about life perfectly led, but it's about our not giving up on the process and believing that there's a much bigger picture to God's purpose for all of us than our ability to screw it all up. We wouldn't need a Savior if everybody did everything right."

5. TRY TO LEARN SOMETHING NEW EVERY DAY.

I believe that God expects his people to be involved in a lifetime quest for wisdom and knowledge. I also believe that if you truly want to be a success in life, you must never stop learning. That's why I try to take advantage of every opportunity to learn something new. For example, when

I'm running in a marathon, I carry some Scripture verses along with me and try to memorize them during the race. When I'm traveling, I take advantage of time on airplanes and in hotel rooms by reading and listening to audio tapes. Whether it's something simple, such as a new word, or something important, such as a long passage from the Bible, I try to learn something new every day.

Brian Tracy, who is one of the world's most successful motivational authors and speakers, says, "Your ability to think well and act effectively depends on the quality and quantity of knowledge and ideas available to you. You must continually feed your mind to develop more of your potential."

He goes on to say, "The highest paid people in America read two to three hours each day to keep current and improve their minds. But if you read only one hour per day from a good book that helps you to be better at your job, that would be enough."

In addition to learning new things, keep your mind sharp. Don't dull it with things like alcohol, marijuana, or watching too much television, surfing the net, or playing video games.

6. Find joy in giving.

Jesus said, "Give, and it will be given to you" (Luke 6:38). This doesn't mean that we ought to have the attitude of "I'm going to give so I can get." But rather, we should give selflessly and know God will bless us for it.

Some people teach that if you give money, God will bless you by giving it back to you. Maybe. But not necessarily.

I think that what Jesus is talking about goes much deeper than material things. It's generally true that people who are "givers" do better in life than people who are "takers." Givers have more peace of mind, more joy, more blessings of all kinds.

Perhaps you've heard this example before, but I still think it's one of the best illustrations of the importance of giving. The Dead Sea is a lifeless, desolate place. Nothing lives in its waters. Hence the name "Dead Sea." Why is it dead? Because although several rivers run into it, none flow out of it. It takes and takes, but doesn't give. As a result, the water is stagnant. To give is to live. To refuse to give is to die.

But don't just take it from me. After being seriously injured in an accident in 1999, author Stephen King had plenty of time to think about the really important matters in life. Recently, in *Family Circle* magazine, he wrote:

> We all know that life is ephemeral, but on that particular day and in the months that followed, I got a painful but extremely valuable look at life's simple backstage truths. We come in naked and broke. We may be dressed when we go out, but we're just as broke. Warren Buffett? Going to go out broke. Bill Gates? Going out broke. Tom Hanks? Going out broke. Steve King? Broke. Not a crying dime. . . .
>
> A life of giving—not just money, but time and spirit—repays. It helps us remember that we may be going out broke, but right now we're doing OK. Right now we have the power to do great good for others and for ourselves.
>
> So I ask you to begin giving, and to continue as you begin. I think you'll find in the end that you got far more than you ever had, and did more good than you ever dreamed.

The only thing I can add is this thought from Senator Don Nickles of Oklahoma: "Greet everybody you see with love in your heart. It's contagious."

7. SET GOALS AND PLAN AHEAD.

A few years ago, I had one of the greatest adventures of my life when I joined a group of people climbing Mount Rainier. Before I left for the trip, I figured that when I got to the mountain, I'd get a crash course in mountain climbing and then I'd be ready to go.

It didn't work that way. Instead I discovered that we were going to spend an entire day learning how to climb that mountain. At first, I was impatient. I wanted to get on with the climb. But the more I learned, the more I saw the importance of preparation. If we had started climbing before we were fully prepared, the situation would've ended in disaster. I hate to think about what might've happened to us on that mountain if we hadn't taken the time to learn how to do things right.

You see, if you want to get somewhere, it's important to have a map. And realistic, specific goals will serve as your road map through life. Otherwise, you might end up like the children of Israel, who wandered around the desert for forty years trying to make it to the Promised Land!

Here are some important things to know about setting goals:

- Your goals should be in writing. This will help you refine them so they are as succinct and accurate as possible.

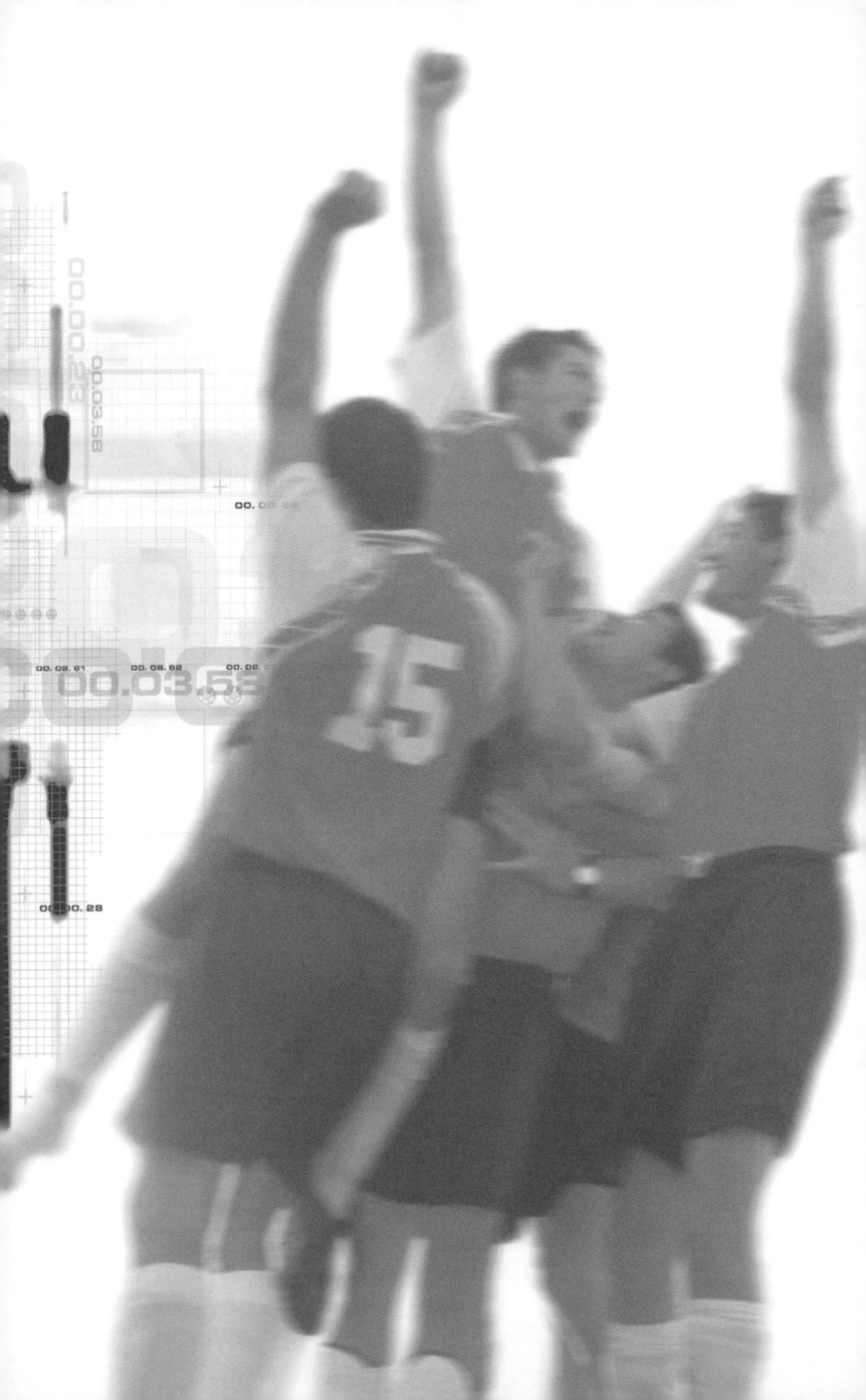

- Each goal should have one specific objective. Again, it's important to be as clear as possible so you know exactly what it is you hope to achieve.
- Each goal should be measurable. That way, you'll know when it's been achieved.
- Each goal should have a specific deadline attached to it. Otherwise, you might wind up moving it from week to week, month to month, and year to year without ever accomplishing it.
- Your goals must be realistic. It won't do you much good to set goals that have nothing to do with your abilities, skills, and opportunities. For example, it would be downright silly if someone who is tone deaf set the goal of becoming an opera singer.

8. Seek greatness through servanthood.

In Jesus' day, the roads through Palestine were dusty, rutted paths used by sheep, goats, and cattle, as well as human travelers. Because the people who walked these roads wore sandals, their feet and ankles were often caked with dirt and mud. Thus, whenever visitors entered a home, one of the first acts of hospitality was to kneel down in front of the visitors and wash their feet.

Oh, the owners of the house didn't do it themselves. It was too degrading. The job fell to the least of the household servants—unless the owners were too poor to have servants.

So you can imagine how shocked Jesus' twelve disciples were when, during his last supper prior to his crucifixion, "he got up from the meal, took off his outer clothing, and wrapped a towel around his waist. After that, he poured water into a basin and began to wash his disciples' feet, drying them with the towel that was wrapped around him" (John 13:4–5).

Through his actions, Jesus was driving home a point he had made earlier:

> "You know that the rulers of the Gentiles lord it over them, and their high officials exercise authority over them. Not so with you. Instead, whoever wants to become great among you must be your servant, and whoever wants to be first must be your slave—just as the Son of Man did not come to be served, but to serve, and to give his life as a ransom for many."
>
> MATTHEW 20:25–26

Being a servant didn't come easy in first century Palestine, and it doesn't come easy in twenty-first century America. Common knowledge says to "take what you want" and "be tough, or else people will walk all over you."

But Jesus says, "Whoever wants to be the greatest of all must be the slave of all" (Mark 10:44 TLB). Just think what the world would be like if we were all willing to wash one another's feet!

9. DON'T LIMIT YOURSELF.

Carly Fiorina, chief executive officer of Hewlett-Packard, said, "Understand that the only limits that really matter are those you put on yourself or that a business puts on itself.

If everyone obeyed the
Ten Commandments
and followed the
Golden Rule, there
would be no problems
in the world.

RONALD REAGAN

Most people and most businesses are capable of far more than they realize."

Is this true? Well, consider the fact that today's junior high school athletes are competing at a level that would've landed them among the top finishers in the Olympics at the turn of the century. Why has this happened? Because, as author John Maxwell says, "During the last one hundred years, athletes have invariably discovered new ways to run faster, jump higher and throw farther. Success, therefore, has meant not merely doing what previous champions have done, but pioneering new methods."

It's true that if you keep on doing things the same old way, you'll get the same old results. The first time Thomas Edison tried to invent the electric lightbulb, he failed. If his second attempt had been exactly the same as his first, he would've failed in exactly the same way. But he kept trying something new until he got it right.

And don't listen to people who say you can't do something. There've always been plenty of those negative folks around, and there always will be. But almost every great invention has been made in spite of this type of person.

In 1947, aviation "experts" said that the sound barrier couldn't be broken—at least not without major damage to the airplane and pilot involved. But Chuck Yeager broke the barrier, reaching a speed of 700 miles per hour, and both he and his aircraft came away unscathed. Three weeks later, he reached a speed of 1,612 miles per hour.

I believe that when you limit yourself, you're insulting God. After all, he's the one who made you in his image. I love what former NFL star Bill Glass has to say about this:

Every one of us performs in a manner consistent with our own self-image. And our self-image can't ever be all it should be until we see our potential the way God sees it. We should try to get a glimpse of what God thinks we're capable of and base our goal-setting and scorekeeping on that. All human beings think small compared to God. He says, "According to your faith be it unto you" (Matt. 9:29). In essence, he is saying, "The only thing holding you back is your lack of faith."

10. KEEP YOUR EYES ON THE PRIZE.

In other words, remember why you're here. Look at it this way. You're *not* here

- to earn a billion dollars
- to become internationally famous
- to have other people look up to you and respect you
- to have other people serve you

Some—or all—of these things may happen to you, but they shouldn't be the primary purpose of your existence. Instead, you *are* here

- to serve and glorify God
- to tell other people about Jesus

A person who wants to be a true success in life should strive to remember why he or she is here, and then live accordingly. Nothing else matters. After all, this life is only the exhibition season—a brief trial run for the real life that begins after we die. We must let God use us to become the best we can be.

You might say, "God would never use me." Oh, yes, he would! As Pastor John MacArthur says, "He uses ordinary people who have all the struggles, strengths and weaknesses of people like us. It's not what you are that's important; it's what you are willing to become."

As you go through life trusting that God will help you become the person you're meant to be, you may find that he doesn't always give you exactly what you want. But he *will* always give you what you need!

An anonymous Confederate soldier wrote these words during the Civil War:

> I asked God for strength that I might achieve.
> I was made weak that I might learn humbly to obey.
> I asked God for health that I might do greater things.
> I was given infirmity that I might do better things.
> I asked for riches that I might be happy.
> I was given poverty that I might be wise.
> I asked for power that I might have the praise of men.
> I was given weakness that I might feel the need of God.
> I asked for all things that I might enjoy life.
> I was given life that I might enjoy all things.
> I got nothing I asked for, but everything I hoped for . . .
> Almost despite myself, my unspoken prayers were answered.
> I am among all men most richly blessed.

God knows what's best for you. Always. So relax and trust him.

A FEW
FINAL WORDS

BEFORE WE END our journey together, I'd like to pass on a few words of wisdom from my friend Ken Miksell, who runs a Christian television station in Orlando. Here is Ken's philosophy of life, which is very much worth following:

> **Live Longer.** By eating properly, by getting proper amounts of exercise and rest, by doing what you can to take care of your body.
>
> **Live Better.** Seek wisdom and knowledge so that you can improve every area of your life—your marriage, your performance at work, your skills as a parent, etc.
>
> **Live Forever.** Be certain that you have accepted the salvation offered by Jesus Christ.

I can't think of a better philosophy to live by. Nor can I think of three better words than these: Can. Will. Now.

Can. Can you do it? Of course you can! You can do all things through Christ who strengthens you.

Will. Will you use the abilities and skills God has given you? Only you can decide.

Now. Many people never get around to doing the things that are most important in life. When will you begin to step in the direction of your dreams? Do yourself a favor. Do it now!

Pat Williams lives in Winter Park, Florida, and is senior vice president of the NBA's Orlando Magic. He has forty years of professional sports experience, has written twenty-two books, including *Secrets from the Mountain* and *A Lifetime of Success,* and is one of America's most sought-after motivational speakers. Pat and his wife, Ruth, are the parents of nineteen children, fourteen of whom have been adopted from four foreign countries.

If you would like to contact Pat Williams directly, please call him on his direct line at (407) 916-2404 or e-mail him at pwilliams@rdvsports.com. Mail can be sent to the following address:

Pat Williams
c/o RDV Sports
8701 Maitland Summit Boulevard
Orlando, FL 32810

If you would like to contact Pat Williams regarding speaking engagements, please contact his assistant, Melinda Ethington. She can be reached at the above address or on her direct number at (407) 916-2454. Requests can also be faxed to (407) 916-2986 or e-mailed to methington@rdvsports.com.

We would love to hear from you. Please send your comments about this book to Pat Williams at the above address.